INDOOR
Water Garden
DESIGN

INDOOR
Water Garden
DESIGN

YVONNE REES
Consultant:
NICK FLETCHER

All inquiries to be addressed to:
Barron's Educational Series, Inc.
250 Wireless Boulevard
Houppauge, NY 11788
http://wwwbarronseduc.com

Library of Congress Catalog Card Number 2001093442

International Standard Book Number 0-7641-5374-9

QUAR.INGA

Conceived, designed, and produced by:
Quarto Publishing plc
The Old Brewery
6 Blundell Street
London N7 9BH

Senior project editor	Nicolette Linton
Senior art editor	Penny Cobb
Text editors	Selina Mumford, Pat Farrington
Designer	Tanya Devonshire-Jones
Illustrators	Ann Savage, Julian Baker, Kuo Kang Chen, chrisorr.com, Sherri Tay, John Woodcock
Photographers	Ian Howes, Paul Forrester
Picture research	Sandra Assersohn
Indexer	Pamela Ellis
Art director	Moira Clinch
Publisher	Piers Spence

Manufactured by Regent Publishing Services Ltd, Hong Kong
Printed by Leefung-Asco Printers Ltd, China

9 8 7 6 5 4 3 2 1

Author's acknowledgements

Grateful thanks to James Kerswell and Angus Jamieson for their technical advice, and to Nikki for her good humor and patience.

◀ PREVIOUS PAGE
A stylish carved stone wall spout by Michael Cedar is internally lit by fiberoptics to make a superb focal point in the home.

contents

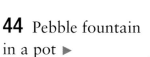

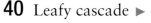

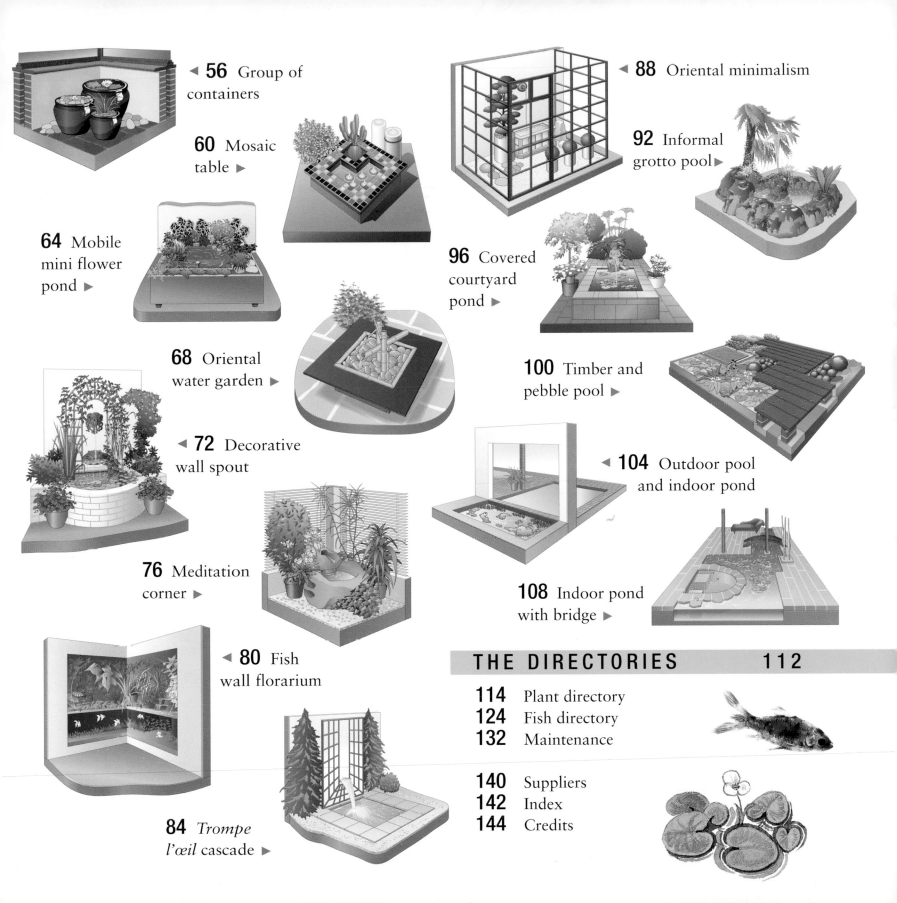

▶ A classic lion's head wall spout cascades into a raised indoor pond.

◀ Small fountains and miniature aquatic plants can be used to create fascinating container gardens.

introduction

Isolepsis cernua

We all know that a water feature in the garden, whether the tiniest trickling spout or gleaming pond, offers ever-changing enjoyment for the eyes and ears; that it is the perfect antidote to stressful, modern living and a great design tool. It is not surprising then that many of us are beginning to bring those benefits indoors, too. The conservatory garden is an obvious place to install a small pool, a modest wall spout, or even a rocky cascade. But tiny tabletop fountains, bubbling urns, even a large sunken pool, can be used to enhance other areas of the home, providing they are imaginatively designed and sensibly installed. The interior design possibilities for water gardening are endless and can be incorporated into any room you choose: if not within a living or dining area, then perhaps making a stylish welcome in the entrance hall or transforming a heated conservatory into a tropical paradise.

▲ This terra-cotta feature would add life to a kitchen.

The smallest features will fit anywhere there is a level surface and a convenient electrical point, adding sound and sparkle to a room: a miniature tabletop fountain in the style of a whimsical waterwheel, or an earthenware pitcher pouring water into a bowl, makes a fine ornament and may include lighting elements, even aromatic oils, to increase its therapeutic benefits. Floor-standing pots and barrels scale up this concept as home for mini-ponds, bubble fountains, and self-contained fountains and cascades. Other great space-savers include wall spouts, where a classical head, a modern sculpture, or even a humble, old-fashioned tap, might trickle water into a small bowl or basin. Sited in an alcove, it doesn't take a lot of skill and imagination to work this theme into a full-size grotto, if you like the gothic look.

For the more ambitious indoor water gardener, there are ponds—whether a small, raised geometric pool, easily stood in the corner, surrounded by houseplants and incorporating a wide flat edging for a seat; or large, formal, sunken ponds, architecturally designed and specially built into the home, maybe even linked to a swimming pool or an outdoor ornamental pond, by floor to ceiling glass doors or windows. You could create an informal jungle pool complete with exotic plants and tropical fish, or a restful area for meditation with bamboo, water, stone, and glass.

I am sure the pictures and projects in this book will fire up your imagination to include water somewhere in your home, especially when you consider the fringe benefits of being able to grow a collection of more tender aquatic and marginal plants such as night-scented water lilies, or the pleasure of keeping exotic fish. Yet these are not the only benefits of an indoor water feature. Positioned near a window, or artificially lit with spotlights, uplighters, or underwater lamps, it can really add life and sparkle to a room. Moving water features such as fountains and cascades offer the additional benefits of sound and

▲ Where space is limited, why not consider a vertical feature like this stylish cascade?

▼ Water can be a wonderful design tool for modern interiors.

Comet

movement and are believed to have therapeutic benefits too: not just because they are soothing, but for the extra oxygen they release into the atmosphere, and the increased levels of humidity they encourage (a valuable consideration in modern centrally-heated homes). There is even medical evidence to suggest that such a feature could be desirable for people with respiratory problems. Water in the conservatory can also be considered beneficial, where many plants will not thrive if the conditions are too hot and dry.

Primarily, though, we design water features for their stylish good looks and the great planting opportunities they offer. Importantly, they must suit surrounding features and the overall style and atmosphere of your home. Natural materials tend to look best: timber, stone, glass, and ceramics are excellent companions for water and plants, and can be played down or dressed up with stains, paints, and ornamental

Iris pseudacorus

▲ Pebble fountains add interest to a room without taking up too much space.

◄ Transform a sunroom or conservatory into a delightful indoor water garden.

A self-contained fountain in an urn can be stood among pots and tubs of indoor foliage plants.

Nephrolepis exaltata 'Bostoniensis', the Boston fern

Primula

Carex cornica 'Snowline'

▲ Bamboo, stone, and water are perfect companions for an oriental-style interior.

decoration as required, to suit your furnishing scheme. That said, good construction and practical maintenance are equally important if your feature is to remain looking good and not cause problems with leaks and spillage. For more ambitious projects, especially indoor sunken pools, you are advised to enlist the help of a qualified architect or construction engineer; certainly get the advice of a qualified electrician where underwater electricity and nearby connections are involved. Bear in mind, too, that larger features will be heavy, so you may need to consider whether the floor is strong enough to take the weight. Reinforce floor joists if necessary. The materials used and construction must be of the highest quality to ensure there is no risk of soil or water spillage, especially if you have adjacent soft furnishings. This will also guarantee the feature lasts well and keeps maintenance tasks to a minimum—it is recommended that you tackle plant and water maintenance regularly and install any necessary filters, cleaners, and oxygenators, to prevent problems building up. Consider, too, the safety aspect if you have elderly or young members of the household and modify your ideas accordingly. Features contained within a pot or which employ a concealed sump remove any risk of accidentally slipping, tripping, or drowning.

Whatever feature you choose, a little careful planning and the right construction techniques should ensure your indoor water garden gives you years of pleasure and enjoyment.

▲ Tiered barrels create a taller, more dramatic fountain effect.

◄ A large wide-topped pottery container is ideal for a multi-pot cascade, pebbles, and plants.

Clematis

the essentials

A good-looking, successful water feature not only requires inspiration, but also a touch of technical know-how. The following pages will help you to choose the style of indoor water feature that's best for your home, show you how it should be installed, and guide you toward the right liners, pumps, filters, fountains, and lights.

◀ Tying bamboo to create an oriental-style water feature.

before you start

When it comes to design and installation, creating an indoor garden is very much the same as gardening outdoors. You must consider making a good focal point, positioning your plants according to size and need, and take into consideration the surrounding environment and features.

The difference, of course, is that here you are in control of the elements, and the plants can flourish without fear of frost or violent storms. You can water, feed, and de-bug in comfort whatever the time of year or weather, potentially keeping the plants in peak condition. If you choose to make your garden in a room such as a sunroom or conservatory, you also have the wonderful opportunity to create the right conditions for a special group of plants: perhaps a cool fernery fringing a shady grotto-type rocky cascade, an orchid house complete with tinkling fountain, or a steamy jungle of tropical plants around a fishpond.

◀ A freestanding water feature makes a fine focal point among a collection of dramatic foliage plants.

▲ A decorative tabletop fountain provides all the pleasure of moving water in the minimum of space.

ADVANTAGES AND DISADVANTAGES

The downside of indoor gardening is that should you forget to water there will be no chance shower of rain to keep your plants alive, pests and disease can proliferate in a closed environment if not spotted early enough, and plants may die in summer simply through lack of shading and ventilation, or be frosted in winter. It is important to remember that, however natural it looks, the indoor garden remains an artificial environment. You need to be vigilant to make the garden work efficiently or employ automatic maintenance systems such as watering, heating, and venting.

Whichever area of the home you are planning to enhance with a water feature or water garden, it is a good idea to assess the advantages and limitations before you start so that your plans can be amended accordingly. Even a small, freestanding fountain bowl or tabletop ornament in the lounge or hallway must be positioned where it won't spoil your furniture or be at risk of getting knocked off; it will require close access to an electrical outlet too. If you want to incorporate plants in your theme, before choosing the room for your garden assess the available light and year-round temperature, as these will make a big difference to your final selection. An ambitious conservatory or sunroom installation will require many aspects to be thought through in advance, such as ease of construction, shading, watering, heating, and humidity. Before a large water feature is installed a structural survey may need to be carried out.

WATER, BUT WHERE?

Unless you have set your heart on a certain water feature and know exactly where you want to position it, the concept of an indoor water garden may still be an exciting idea that you have no idea how to put into practice. Maybe you are attracted to its stunning visual possibilities as part of your interior design scheme, or feel its therapeutic and anti-stress benefits may improve your quality of life.

The quickest and simplest way to introduce the sight and sound of moving water into any room is to buy a pretty tabletop fountain. These are available in a huge range of designs from the whimsically ornamental to sculptural pieces of great style and elegance, and come complete with pump and electrical plug. The fountain will be made of ceramic or metal, and may incorporate mosses, bark, plants, and even lighting. All you have to do is find a level surface to put the fountain on, fill the reservoir with water, and plug it in.

If you prefer something more individual, you can create your own indoor fountain using a miniature pump (available from garden centers and aquatic retailers) and any suitable bowl, jug, pebbles, or ornaments. A fountain can make a fine focal point in the living room, a conversation piece in the dining room, and a relaxing addition to the bedroom. Some designs suggest a certain location; for example a bronzed mermaid spilling water into a shell-encrusted bowl is perfect for the bathroom and the classic little brown jug pouring into a bowl makes the ideal kitchen companion. Formal pools and/or fountains in entrance halls have long been used to make a coolly elegant welcome for classical, Mediterranean, and Southwest homes, but tabletop features offer a good compromise for today's smaller houses and apartments.

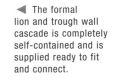

◀ The formal lion and trough wall cascade is completely self-contained and is supplied ready to fit and connect.

▼ Fountain masks, like this Green Man, are available in a wide range of classical designs.

WALL-MOUNTED WATER FEATURES

A more permanent, architectural effect can be achieved by using a wall-mounted moving water feature. These can be found as spouting heads (frequently a traditional lion, a cherub, putti, or gargoyles) that trickle water into a bowl or trough below; there are also more unusual limited edition pieces produced by artists and sculptors. Spouting heads may be made of stone, lead, bronze, ceramic, or even plastic, which is light and easy to handle and manufactured to look like stone or marble. These come self-contained and all you have to do is screw the fountain to the wall using the bracket supplied, conceal the piping between the spout and bowl, and connect it to a convenient electrical source.

You can create your own effect, perhaps with an old tap or wall-mounted sculpture pouring water into a bowl, trough, or wooden tub. If your chosen receptacle is not waterproof, line it with PVC or butyl pond liner. The wall-mounted fountain makes an eye-catching feature in an entrance hall or conservatory, but may even suit a bathroom or bedroom, depending on your style of decoration.

◀ Water cascading onto pebbles in a glass brick trough will transform a dull conservatory into a place of drama.

INDOOR PONDS AND POOLS

Self-contained spouts and fountains can offer the sight and sound of moving water and are both attractive and convenient, but for a little more effort, there is nothing to stop you from creating a pond or pool—complete with plants and fish if you like—within your home. It may be raised or sunken: a formal mosaic-lined, highly decorative feature; an ultramodern architectural statement in glass or Perspex; an informal log-edged corner pond surrounded by plants; or even a total jungle pool and cascade half hidden behind a profusion of exotics. You will find that simple shapes and designs tend to work best. With central heating, daylight bulbs and fluorescent tubes, filters, pumps, automatic timers and ventilation, plus humidifiers and dehumidifiers, you can create exactly the environment you require, even in dark corners or cold rooms. If koi are your passion, you may want to consider an indoor as well as an outdoor pool, possibly interlinked and custom-built with filters, heaters, and drains to satisfy the rather exacting needs of these fishes.

▶ Rigid preformed pond and cascade shapes are ideal for indoor use.

CONSTRUCTING A RAISED INFORMAL CORNER POND

There is nothing to stop you having an informal pool complete with fish and aquatic plants in the corner of your sitting room or conservatory. Faced with stone or timber, even a raised pond will look natural. This design could be adapted to create a wilder effect with a rocky backdrop and water cascade built up the rear wall, and a jungle of exotic plants in containers around the perimeters.

① Mark out the shape you require in a corner of the room using string or hose. Stand back and check that the size and shape look right. Using concrete building blocks, build up and cement them to the floor all the way round, including the back of the pond.

② Lay pieces of discarded carpet or pond underlay inside the pool to cushion the liner.

③ Lay a piece of flexible PVC or butyl liner over the pool, overlapping the sides, and slowly fill the pool with water using a hose, allowing the weight of the water to pull the liner into place.

④ Drill holes into the blocks with a concrete bit. Insert rawl plugs and lay the timber edging roll vertically around the outside of the pond. Screw the roll to the blocks between the timber slats. Trim away any excess liner.

⑤ Lay log slices around the rim for a neat finish, securing with galvanized screws.

POINTS TO REMEMBER

● This style of pool is only suited to rooms with a solid concrete floor. If your floor is timber, you will have to use a preformed liner (see page 18).

● Make sure the flexible liner is completely concealed by your facing material and the overhanging coping stones or timber.

● Install special grow lights to ensure plants flourish in this corner location.

● Take great care when installing, not to snag or puncture the liner as a leak could be disastrous indoors.

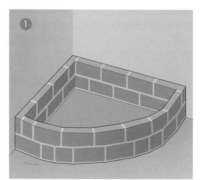

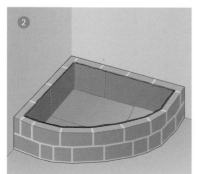

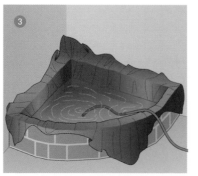

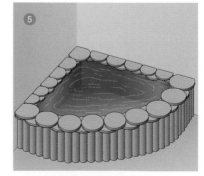

Unless you are prepared to dig up the floor, or are still at the planning stages with a new house, a raised pond is the more practical option. For a small pond this may be as simple as an old barrel or a terra-cotta urn, lined and planted with miniature water lilies and tiny reeds or sedges. Larger ponds can be created using a preformed liner which is available in a wide range of shapes and sizes, from the sculpted informal look to geometric squares and rectangles. These can be supported by a timber framework and disguised by tiles, mosaic, rough or planed and painted timber, and even stone or slabs to achieve the look you want. You could even enjoy the soft gurgle of a bubble fountain in a corner of the sitting room or conservatory, with the sump hidden under the floor or within a raised platform big enough to support a range of additional container plants.

▶ A raised pond enlivened by a wall-mounted fountain is quick and easy to construct.

INSTALLING A RAISED FORMAL POND

A raised pond avoids any need for excavation and using a preformed liner will give it stability, as well as make it easier to complete the pond. A formal style often suits an interior location best and can be faced with a decorative finish such as ceramic tiles or mosaic. Alternatively, timber can be painted or stained to suit other furnishing details in the room. You will find a wide range of shapes and sizes of liners at your local aquatic center.

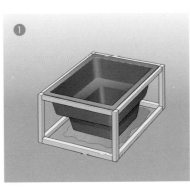

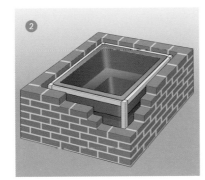

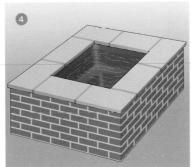

① Place the fiberglass pool on a cushioned layer of sand if the floor is concrete or a piece of carpet or pond underlay if it consists of boards. Build a simple wooden frame around the pool to support it; bolt or screw it into the floor for extra stability. Check it is level using a piece of flat, warp-free timber and a level.

② Face the support structure with your chosen material, bringing it level with the top of the pond.

③ Fill the pool slowly using a hose, and simultaneously pack loft insulation material or Vermiculite between the liner and the facing boards. You may need to push it down with a cane.

④ Overlap the top of the pool with coping tiles, slabs, or timber, chosen to match the sides.

POINTS TO REMEMBER

● The pool has to be built *in situ* for stability. Once filled with water, plants, and possibly fish, it would be too heavy to move.

● Timber or stone slabs around the top edge could create pool-side seating as well as disguise the liner.

● A raised pool such as this could be incorporated with other built-in features such as a seating unit, shelving, and storage.

● When choosing a preformed fiberglass liner, allow for it to be quite a bit larger once it is supported and faced.

● Check that your floor is strong enough to take the weight of the pool, water, and plants.

If you are prepared to incorporate a below-ground pond in your new house design, or excavate the existing floor, the effects can be stunning. Again you may use a preformed shape for lining, but a strong, flexible liner or even concrete if you have the skill, offers more scope in design. You will find all these ideas explored in this book, together with the practical information you need to construct and maintain them.

◀ Preformed fiberglass ponds come in a wide range of formal and informal shapes and sizes.

CONSTRUCTING A SUNKEN FORMAL POND IN AN EXISTING FLOOR

This is not an easy project to tackle. It will involve a large amount of upheaval and will breach any existing damp proof membrane which will have to be replaced. But the final effect of a highly decorative formal sunken pond can make a stunning focal point for a living area, conservatory, or entrance hall.

▲ A thick, soft underlay material will protect flexible liners from damage.

❶ Mark out the area of the pool using tape or a marker pen. Use a set square to ensure right angles at the corners.

❷ Cut out the floorboards if necessary, then cut out the concrete slightly larger than you need using a diamond-tipped cutter.

❸ Tidy up the excavation and line the hole with insulation or underlay, if it is very rough, before lining it with plastic damp-proof membrane. Make sure you have sufficient liner to cover the sides and base in one piece.

❹ Use concrete building blocks and cement to line the inside of the hole, staggering the joins for strength. When the concrete has set, trim the membrane to fit around the top edge.

❺ Render the base and sides of the pool with a stiff 4:1 concrete mix to which waterproofer has been added. Smooth with a float and leave it to dry.

❻ Paint, tile, or mosaic the inside of the pool incorporating a decorative edge around its rim.

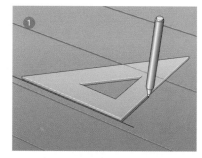

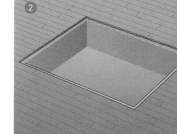

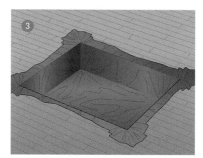

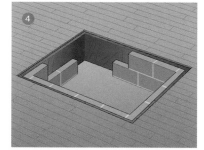

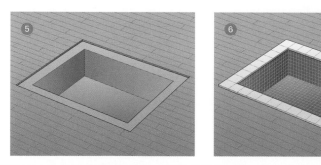

POINTS TO REMEMBER

● A sunken pool is not recommended for rooms used by children or elderly members of the family, who may be unsteady on their feet.

● Diamond-tipped cutters are available from hire stores: you may need to purchase replacement discs if the job is a big one, so allow for this in your budget.

● Always wear a mask, gloves, and goggles when using cutting equipment.

● If the pond is to be used for keeping koi, it would be a good idea to incorporate a bottom drain in your design (see page 128).

MOVING WATER FEATURES

Much of the pleasure of owning a water feature is the sound of moving water via a fountain, bubbler, or cascade. There is no reason you cannot enjoy these features indoors as part of a pool, providing you set the flow so that the water does not splash over the sides where it may cause damage and require constant refilling. For this you need an electric pump; a low-voltage submersible model should be sufficient, and your local aquatic retailer will be able to advise on size and function. Use it to power a classic fountain spout, or a bell fountain if you want to minimize splash. Alternatively, the fountain outlet can be concealed within an ornamental figure, a sculptural stone, or a pile of pebbles. An ambitious project may involve a rocky backdrop to your pond complete with rolling cascade—providing it is safely constructed and does not splash water. The possibilities for a moving water feature are endless, even indoors.

INSTALLING A BUBBLE FOUNTAIN

▶ A bubble fountain can be used to make an exciting feature from a simple pot or urn.

Bubble fountains add the sound and movement of a major water feature to a room, but because the water reservoir is completely concealed they are safe for pets and children. You may be able to sink the sump beneath a suspended floor. If this is not possible—or you do not wish to excavate—build a platform around it which you can transform into a lushly planted area with bamboos and other architectural plants grown in containers.

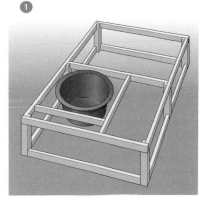

❶ Build a timber framework tall enough to hide the plastic sump, but a larger surface area than you need to accommodate a variety of container-grown plants.

❷ Fix an area of metal mesh over the sump, large enough for a good arrangement of pebbles. Use ceramic tiles glued to hardboard sections or tongue-and-grooved timber stained or painted to match your interior decoration, to create a stylish platform area.

❸ Lift the grid and fill the sump with water. Install the pump and fountain outlet, and connect it to a nearby electrical supply.

❹ Disguise the grid with pebbles and add some height and interest around the feature with large, smooth boulders and dramatic foliage plants such as plants and ferns in tubs or pots.

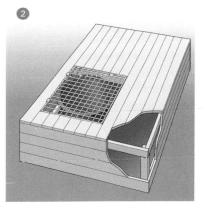

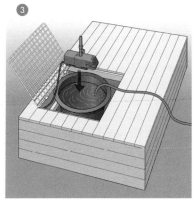

POINTS TO REMEMBER

● Only use well-washed, rinsed stones and pebbles, as any detritus might clog the pump and pollute the water.

● Hinge the metal grid for easy access to the sump.

● A large bored boulder or circular millstone would be an interesting alternative to pebbles.

● Concealed spotlighting would make this a fine feature for a dark corner or an after-dark focal point.

the projects

Whether bold and dramatic, or simply restful, there's a water feature to suit every size and style of indoor setting. The following projects offer inspiration and guidance for a wide range of ideas that could be adapted to your own home, from tabletop fountain to full-scale conservatory garden.

◄ Pale timber decking and white-washed walls are the restful background for this stylish fountain.

self-contained cauldron *fountain*

▲ **1** *Asparagus plumosa* (syn. *Protasparagus plumosus, A. setaceus*) is a delicate, easy-to-grow, climbing perennial whose finely divided fronds create a feathery cloud of light green.

ADVANTAGES

● Self-contained features can be installed virtually anywhere in the home.

● Safer for homes with young children.

● A few large specimen plants create a leafy effect but keep maintenance to a minimum.

This large terra-cotta water feature is available complete with pebbles and pump.

This elegantly self-contained water feature could be installed anywhere in the home or conservatory, provided there is a convenient electrical outlet and sufficient light for plants to grow. In this sunroom extension, russet brickwork and softening greenery create the perfect complementary background for a voluptuously curved terra-cotta cauldron with its gently spilling fountain.

Cascading into a matching pot well-contained within a circle of pebbles, there is no risk of water spills, and the cauldron itself stands on sturdy terra-cotta feet to protect the marble-topped table. It could be installed equally well in a furnished living or dining room, as in a conservatory. A cloud of feathery lime *Asparagus plumosa* spreads out behind like patterned wallpaper, with a slender statue providing extra interest among the foliage. At the fountain's feet, dark, glossy *Monstera* partly hides the sharp lines of the shiny marble and cast-iron legs of the table.

▼ **2** Pebbles always look great with water features where a regular wetting brings out their gloss and subtle color variations. Here they disguise a concealed sump in a freestanding, child-safe water feature, while adding another natural touch in this pleasing combination of pots, plants, and water.

3 Indoor fountains and cascades should be adjusted to cut splash to a minimum. This is not just to reduce the chances of spoiling surrounding features and furnishings, but also to avoid frequent refilling. Make sure your container is large enough, and adjust the fountain nozzle until you get the effect you want.

THE CAST OF CHARACTERS

▼ **④** Terra-cotta has a warm, natural feel, and a selection of items—accompanied by the right plants—will lend a Mediterranean atmosphere to your scheme. Pots, urns, and planters come in all shapes and sizes, and can be coordinated with other terra-cotta features such as troughs, ornaments, and even floor tiles.

▼ *Choisya ternata*, the Mexican orange blossom, is a fine evergreen foliage plant with fresh, glossy foliage (a golden color in variety 'Sundance') and the bonus of small white scented flowers in spring. Sometimes the shrub blooms again in summer.

▶ *Monstera deliciosa*, the Swiss cheese plant, with its giant glossy slit leaves, grows at an impressive rate given warm, bright conditions and high humidity. Reaching a possible height of 10 feet (3m), it needs a trellis or mossy pole once it starts to climb.

▶ *Philodendron scandens*, the sweetheart plant, is another glossy-leaved climber that grows well in bright, warm conditions with high humidity, although it will also thrive in more moderate conditions.

◀ The tree philodendron, *Philodendron bipinnatifidum*, is a striking Brazilian shrub that produces large, glossy butterfly-shaped leaves on long, strong stems.

▶ *Fatshedera lizei* will also produce a tall—6 feet (2m)—plant of interesting glossy foliage. The five-lobed, wavy-edged leaves look particularly good against a painted wall.

◀ *Asparagus setaceus* 'Nana' is a delightful asparagus fern for smaller settings with its delicate, feathery, bright green fronds.

▼ **⑥** *Helxine soleirolii*, baby's tears, makes a tight, creeping mound of tiny leaves, useful for growing beneath taller houseplants.

◀ **⑤** The creeping curly fronds of ferny *Selaginella* do a good job of softening the edges of indoor pots and paving. It is useful in that it prefers shady conditions so grows well beneath other plants, but it does require warmth and high humidity.

SETTING THE SCENE

SELF-CONTAINED FOUNTAIN

Freestanding fountains come in many shapes and styles suitable for indoors or out: if not a terra-cotta cauldron with spilling pot like this one, then perhaps a cascading statue in a stone shell-shaped bowl on a matching pedestal, or an old-fashioned hand pump pouring water into a rustic barrel.

LARGE FOLIAGE PLANTS

When choosing foliage for decorative effect, go for a good blend of dramatic leaf shapes and colors. Here gold, dark green, and bright lime encompass both glossy, waxy leaves and the more delicate effect of feathery foliage.

ORNAMENTAL STATUE

Used sparingly, a piece of statuary, sculpture, or a decorative ornament makes an excellent talking point and secondary focal point, especially when partly concealed by foliage.

TABLE TOP

Raising your feature slightly gives it more prominence and usefully keeps it clear from the main floor. Here, an old cast-iron table makes the perfect indoor/outdoor furniture, with the cool smoothness of its marble slab top providing a pleasing contrast of texture and color.

BEHIND THE SCENES

SELF-CONTAINED FOUNTAIN

Once assembled, a freestanding fountain only needs to be filled with water and the power switched on to be fully functional. If you are planning to get a water feature and you have pets or young children, a model like this one with a concealed sump is ideal.

Choisya ternata

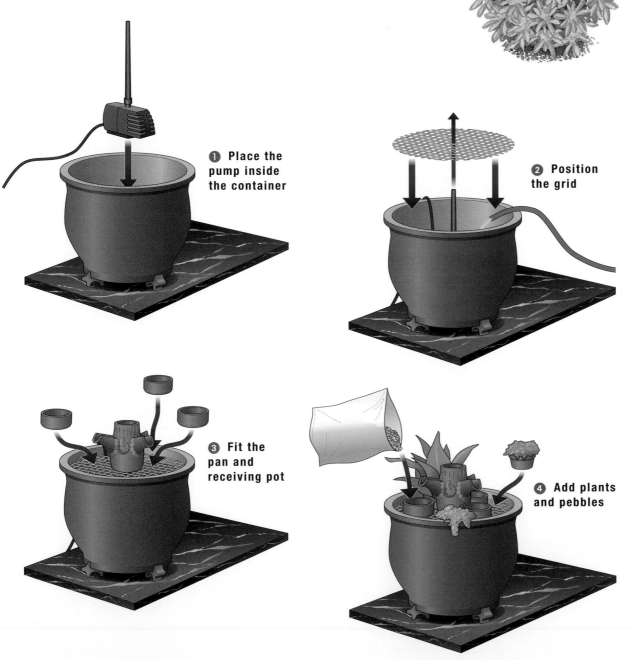

❶ Place the pump inside the container

❷ Position the grid

❸ Fit the pan and receiving pot

❹ Add plants and pebbles

❶ Lift the urn or bowl carefully into position on a stable surface, adjusting the feet if necessary. Place the pump inside the bowl, as recommended by the manufacturer, and run the cable safely to the nearest electrical outlet. Tuck out of sight using the tabletop or surrounding plants and pots.

❷ Position the grid, making sure the fountain outlet coming from the pump rests on top. Fill slowly with water, using a hose.

❸ Lift the terra-cotta pan gently over the fountain outlet and adjust so that it will pour from the spout. Turn on the pump and place the receiving pot in the correct position.

❹ When the fountain is running successfully, add one or two creeping plants in pots to soften the edge of the cauldron, then cover the grid and the base of the pots with pebbles.

Helxine soleirolii

▲ ❶ Miniature pumps are perfect for smaller water features and are available from aquarium suppliers.

herb tray

This window box of traditional herbs has been given extra vitality with a mini bubble fountain in a terra-cotta pot. This creates a point of interest in what can be a rather utilitarian setting, its windowsill position ensuring that the sparkling movement of water catches plenty of sunshine, with the added benefit that the warmth and humidity enhances the natural aroma of the plants.

Much of this feature's charm is due to its natural informality, yet it is the forethought and practical application in its construction that is the key to its success. The size of the box container was determined by the size of the plant pots; the central section was lined with PVC pond liner to accommodate a water feature without leakage; finally the box was painted to match the room. The whole feature has a personal feel—it's up to you to select the herbs you wish to grow. The herbs here have been specially chosen for their culinary usefulness: a savory selection suitable for adding flavor to stews, stuffings, roasts, and sauces.

▲ ❷ Gravel is a good mulch material and is better suited to smaller containers than pebbles or shingle. It is available in a range of colors and sizes.

▲ ❸ Sage, *Salvia officinalis*, has a pungent flavor that needs to be used sparingly, and soft gray-green foliage that looks good beside other plants. There are several interesting, and more tender, variations that are also suited to an indoor windowsill.

ADVANTAGES

● The feature is both attractive and useful, but takes up no space in the room.

● Provides fresh herbs for the kitchen.

● Adds life and interest to a workplace area.

Herbs and other plants can be bought in pots from supermarkets and garden centers, and are easy to replace.

THE CAST OF CHARACTERS

▶ **4** Thyme, *Thymus*, is another herb with a wide range of forms, colors, and flavors, and because it has such tiny leaves and a creeping habit, it is ideal for growing in containers.

▶ **6** Mint, *Mentha*, grows vigorously, so it is best confined to a pot. It has many variegated foliage forms and flavors for creating different combinations and effects.

▶ Coriander, *Coriandrum sativum*, has feathery pungent leaves that make a good contrast to other herbal foliage, and is useful for adding fresh to curries and stir fries.

◀ Oregano, *Origanum*, makes a fine bushy plant with delicate bright green or golden leaves, and attractive purple summer flowers.

◀ **7** Basil, *Ocimum basilicum*, with its warm spicy flavor, is a tender herb well suited to growing indoors. The bush or Greek variety is best for pots as it has a compact habit and small, pointed leaves, but there are many interesting variations worth experimenting with on sunny windowsills.

◀ Chives, *Allium*, with their clumps of bright-green, grasslike foliage, make a fine display in a pot and add a mild onion flavor to salads, soups, and scones.

▶ **5** Rosemary, *Rosmarinus*, is a good contrast to other herbs with its tall, spiky evergreen stems and gray-green color. The flowers are a delightfully delicate blue.

▶ Curry plant, *Helichrysum angustifolium*, is a striking plant with its spiky silver foliage and bright yellow flowers. It gets its name from the spicy aroma of the leaves but is mostly grown as an ornamental plant and is a good foil for other herbs.

▶ Savory, *Satureja*, produces narrow, almost peppery leaves that can be used as a substitute for parsley. The winter savory *S. montana* has tougher, slightly more bitter foliage.

SETTING THE SCENE

WINDOW BOX

Garden suppliers sell a variety of plastic, wooden, and lead planters, specially designed for windowsills, but making your own creates a more individual and practical feature to suit the space. The use of preformed corners makes working with wood or fiberboard quicker and simpler.

BUBBLER

A small bubble fountain can add splash and movement to the smallest of receptacles, and simply requires sufficient headroom and access to a safe electrical point nearby.

TERRA-COTTA POTS

Terra-cotta pots are available in many sizes and styles, from thimble pots to giant urns, and have a rough earthy finish that goes well with aromatic herbs. They also look good with water but, unglazed, they are porous, so allow for this when designing water features.

HERBS

A selection of small-leafed herbs is ideal for a windowsill location, where it can extend the season for fresh flavors well into the winter months. Within the range of herbs available, you will find an excellent choice of foliage shapes and colors.

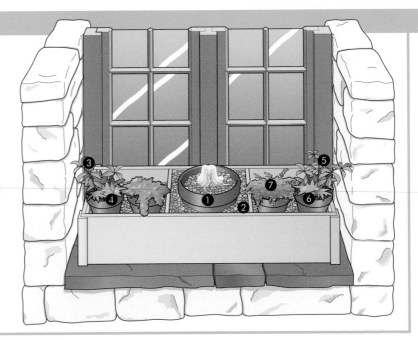

BEHIND THE SCENES

WINDOW BOX WITH WATER FEATURE

Window boxes and similar planters are easy to make using wood or medium-density fiberboard. Paint or stain them to suit your interior decorative scheme for a completely individual creation.

1 Build the compartmentalized box from wood or fiberboard using the height of your plant pots and the width of your windowsill as a guide to size and divisions. The center section will be designed to hold the slightly larger pot that is going to be converted into a water feature. Paint or stain it to the finish of your choice.

2 Line the central section with a piece of flexible pond liner, stapling and trimming for a neat finish.

3 To make the water feature, push a piece of piping through the drainage hole in the bottom of a pot and seal it with silicone. Connect it to a miniature pump and bubble fountain.

4 Fill planting sections with gravel and add water. Place pot fountain in central section.

5 Put an inch (2.5cm) of gravel in the bottom of the planting sections for drainage and add the pots of herbs.

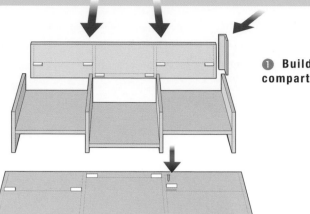

1 Build the compartmentalized box

2 Line the central section

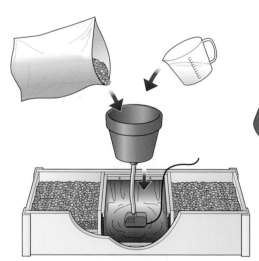

4 Fill planting sections with gravel and add water

3 Seal the pipe pushed through the drainage hole

5 Add gravel to fountain and place pots

POINTS TO REMEMBER

● Don't crop plants too heavily for cooking or they will not recover quickly enough. However, pinching off a few leaves regularly during the growing season will encourage good bushy growth. Feed weekly during the summer.

● Filling the pot and reservoir with gravel for the bubble fountain reduces the amount of water used, and ensures it does not pass through the pot too quickly.

● Install grow light bulbs or strip lights into the windowsill area to keep herbs growing through the shorter days of winter.

● Stencils, stripes, and stick-on moldings can all be used to give your window box an individual look.

leafy
cascade

The natural warmth of terra-cotta is enhanced by a continuous bubbling stream of water flowing over the glass—a charming addition to any kitchen or conservatory.

Bring a touch of moving art into your living room with a self-contained, tabletop water sculpture like this gleaming copper leaf cascade. Installed in an elegant urn and softened by spiky greenery, it makes a superb focal point on a table, shelf, or windowsill, with its strong vertical line and exciting contrast of textures.

The bold copper foliage is sculpted to look like real leaves and has been cleverly arranged so that water spills gently from one to another, providing constant sparkle and shimmer. A discreet pump concealed in the container serves to recycle the water, and needs only to be plugged in and switched on to operate. The urn is wide-topped and full-bellied to balance the dramatic height and breadth of the copper leaves, and also helps to reduce any possibility of splashing. Its soft, blue color is the perfect *verdigris* complement to the copper, and it is topped by a bed of textural larva pebbles, blending gray, blue, and bronze tints.

The plants are lush and green, but are kept under control to prevent them from smothering the feature. Each has been specially chosen for growing in a restricted space and has been planted directly into the container, with its roots wrapped in a piece of nylon stocking filled with aquatic compost.

▲ ❶ *Acorus gramineus* is a miniature version of the sweet flag, *A. calamus*, whose softly curved leaves barely reach 12 inches (30cm) long with 1 inch (25mm) flower spikes. There are also pretty striped varieties.

▲ *Cyperus isocladus* is a dwarf-growing version of the umbrella sedge or papyrus, and features in miniature, the familiar umbel heads rising on long stems among grasslike leaves.

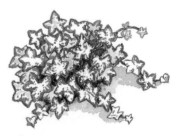

▲ ❷ *Hedera helix*, or ivy, is available in a wide range of leaf shapes and colorings, and is useful for twining around and softening other features. Like other plants in this setting, it would need to be kept in check to maintain the impact of the feature.

THE CAST OF CHARACTERS

▼ *Selaginella kraussiana*, spreading club moss, is an easy-to-grow fern whose spreading stems of tiny bright-green leaves are perfect for covering the edges of pots and containers.

▼ *Pteris cretica* is the Cretan brake fern, a delicate evergreen fern that thrives in moist, indoor conditions. The best known cultivated variety is *'Albolineata'*.

▼ ❸ Houseplant *Cyperus alternifolius 'Gracilis'*, or umbrella plant, should be stood in a water-filled saucer to keep the roots damp where it will produce a fine clump of delicate grasslike bracts like the spokes of an open umbrella.

▲ *Apsplenium trichomanes*, the maidenhair spleenwort, is a bright-green evergreen fern that makes a clump of highly defined, ferny fronds to a height of around 10 inches (25cm).

▼ *Polypodium vulgare*, or adder's fern, is a useful surface-spreading evergreen that grows well in containers.

► Iris with their bold straplike leaves and beautiful butterfly blooms include dwarf varieties suitable for growing in container water gardens.

► Spider plant, *Chlorophytum comosum 'Vittatum',* makes a glossy fountain of shiny, striped foliage that looks good in pots or hanging baskets.

SETTING THE SCENE

SCULPTURE
A small sculptured fountain may cost a little more than a mass-produced tabletop water feature, but will add an element of style, elegance, and excitement to your home interior. There are many interesting and original designs to choose from.

CONTAINER
The right size and style of container is essential to both the esthetic and practical success of the feature, and must be chosen not only to suit your home, but to be in scale and tone with the sculpture, too. The urn must be deep enough to hide the pump, and its surface area should be large enough to take the splash of the cascade.

PLANTS
The plants chosen here are dwarf varieties of lush water species, that not only look appropriate, but also provide an interesting variety of foliage shapes. Alternatively, dramatic foliage plants like ferns, palms, and ivies could be arranged in pots close to the urn, which would produce a similar effect but be easier to maintain.

PEBBLES
Pebbles are the perfect finishing touch, concealing the pump and plant roots, and helping to maintain water clarity. There are many sizes, colors, and textures of stone to choose from in order to complement your fountain, plants, and container; remember that being constantly wet will enhance their color and shine.

BEHIND THE SCENES

SCULPTURE CASCADE IN AN URN

Sculptural fountains and cascades are generally supplied complete with compact pump and fittings, although the container, plants, and pebbles are usually optional. You need to choose carefully to complement both your feature and your home décor.

1 Put the urn in position as it will be too heavy when filled. Place the pump in the bottom and connect the sculpture to the pump as advised.

2 Fold a piece of chicken wire around it to protect it from the plants and pebbles. Fill the container with water.

3 Wrap the roots of the plants gently in a good handful of aquatic potting mix enclosed in a piece of old nylon stocking to prevent spillage and water pollution. Lower the plants carefully into position in the pot.

4 Add the pebbles gradually, using them to hold the plants in position. Take care not to impede the pump. Level the pebbles on the top of the container and switch on the pump.

1 Position the urn and fit the pump

2 Fold chicken wire around the pump and fill the urn with water

---

POINTS TO REMEMBER

● The height of the cascade and relatively small surface area of the container will result in a considerable amount of moisture being lost through evaporation, so you will need to top it off regularly with fresh water.

● Circulating the water will help prevent it from getting stale, but as an extra precaution indoors, add a tablespoon of fine charcoal (filter carbon), available from aquarium stockists, to the water.

● If you are away from home a lot or you don't have much spare time, you could reduce maintenance and keep the feature looking good by replacing the plants with good artificial versions that simply need twining into position and keeping dust free.

● Use a spotlight or place where it will receive plenty of natural light to show this feature off to the best advantage.

3 Prepare the plants to go into the pot

4 Add pebbles and switch on pump

Cyperus isocladus

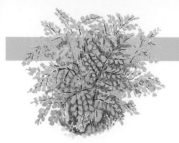

▲ **1** Maidenhair fern, *Adiantum raddianum*, with its delicate black wiry stems of light green, feathery foliage, makes a frothy cloud of foliage perfect for softening more solid features. It thrives in a humid atmosphere, so it is perfect beside indoor ponds and fountains.

pebble fountain
in a pot

▶ **2** Algerian ivy, *Hedera canariensis*, is a vigorous climbing or trailing plant with gray-green variegated foliage. It grows well and is available in a wide range of sizes.

ADVANTAGES

- Safe for children.
- Highly decorative for an indoor setting.
- Low maintenance.

A large ceramic pot fired in earthy tones makes an eye-catching yet restful container for a gentle pebble fountain, cleverly positioned beside the sliding patio doors in a Japanese-inspired interior. The colors are subtle, but an ornamented dragon is visible on the side of the pot that serves to complement the strong Oriental feel created by the large, black-framed doors.

This blend of strong shapes, and the natural colors and textures of stone and ceramic, softened by feathery ferns and trailing ivies, also make an excellent link with stone and plant features viewed in soft focus through the glass in the garden beyond. When the doors are left open in summer, the barriers between indoors and outdoors are completely removed. There are no further distractions other than the gentle movement of the drilled stone fountain on its bed of gleaming wet pebbles: the floor is stone and a nearby container-grown Japanese maple with its sprays of decorative foliage takes the place of curtains or blinds. The overall effect is one of harmony and relaxation for all the senses.

▼ Gravel is an easy-to-maintain mulch material for a pebble fountain feature and can be used to create a variety of complementary effects.

A bubble fountain can be adapted to all kinds of stone ornament, like this striking dome feature.

THE CAST OF CHARACTERS

▶ The Japanese maple, *Acer palmatum*, makes a small tree or shrub with delicate, feathery foliage in shades of bronze, purple, or maroon. There are many cultivars, including miniature forms suitable for planting in containers. This is essentially a garden plant so pots should be taken outside regularly.

▼ In large, deeper features like this floor-standing pot, you need some kind of support to hold the pebbles near the rim and to protect the pump. A wire mesh or framework will have to be constructed to fit inside the pot.

▼ Boston fern, *Nephrolepis exaltata* 'Bostoniensis', makes a vigorous clump of strong but graceful, bright green fronds and is a fine specimen plant. It prefers warm, shady conditions.

▲ ④ Plush vine, *Mikania ternate*, looks like a soft-leafed ivy with unusual sage-green coloring and purple stems. It can be grown as a trailing or climbing plant and is a good foil for paler foliage plants.

▼ ③ Ceramic pots make great containers for plants or water and look equally good indoors, in a conservatory, or on a patio. If your chosen pot is too porous or has a drainage hole in the bottom, you may have to insert a molded plastic pot as a liner if you want to convert it to a water feature.

◀ ⑤ Emerald fern, *Asparagus densiflorus*, makes arching fronds of delicate fernlike foliage. It thrives in moist conditions and is excellent for softening harder features.

◀ Strawberry geranium, *Saxifraga stolonifera*, has striking white-veined leaves with red undersides and produces hanging stems of tiny plantlets. It is a fine plant for cooler positions, where it will quickly grow to a height of about 8 inches (20cm).

SETTING THE SCENE

ORNAMENTAL CONTAINER

Ceramic containers come in many sizes and designs for creating indoor water features. Buy the complete kit, or put together your own using components from your local aquatic supply store. It is important to find a pot or urn large enough to create sufficient effect and to conceal the pump. Raising it up on a plinth or table might give a smaller container greater prominence.

BUBBLE FOUNTAIN

Pebble fountains use a bubbler driven by a low-voltage submersible pump concealed in the pot. Here it has been connected to a larger drilled stone (available from pond suppliers) among the pebbles to increase the effect.

PEBBLES

Pebbles usually have to be purchased separately, even when buying the fountain in kit form, so allow for this when calculating costs. The stones must be well washed to keep dirt and debris from polluting the water or blocking the pump.

PLANTING

Soft, natural foliage plants are the best companions for natural features like this one: ferns, ivies—even palms for a more exotic effect—offer a wide variety of interesting shapes and subtle color variations, and also thrive in the more humid conditions around a water feature.

BEHIND THE SCENES

PEBBLE FOUNTAIN IN A POT

The beauty of a pebble fountain is that it is completely contained: it looks good and makes no mess, wherever you choose to site it. This is a feature that looks especially effective if lighted at night, so try to incorporate a spotlight or uplighter hidden by surrounding foliage in your design plans.

Strawberry geranium

❶ Put the empty pot in position, allowing some space behind for plants if in a corner site. Line if the container is not watertight by inserting a slightly smaller container.

❷ Place the pump in the bottom of the pot, propped on a brick or block if it needs additional support. Take the cable to the nearest electrical outlet as unobtrusively as possible. Trailing plants are useful for hiding cables.

❸ Cut a piece of galvanized wire mesh to fit inside the pot about 6 inches (15cm) below the rim and suspend, using wire or butcher's hooks (S hooks) hooked around the rim. Arrange the fountain outlet pipe to come through the center of the mesh. Fill with water.

❹ Position the drilled stone in the middle of the mesh, and fix the fountain outlet pipe in line with the exit hole. Turn on the pump and adjust until you are pleased with the effect.

❺ Place the rest of the pebbles around the fountain stone and add a few softening plants.

POINTS TO REMEMBER

● Once filled with water and stones the pot will be heavy, so try to place it in its final position before filling. If moving the feature is unavoidable, consider placing it on a low cart with castors instead of directly onto the floor.

● You need not buy a drilled stone for the fountain feature: allowing the water to simply bubble through the pebbles can be equally effective.

● Never use stones found in the garden without scrubbing them and disinfecting them, as they may pollute the water.

● Make sure any electrical outlets are far enough away not to be at risk from water or soil splashes.

❶ **Insert watertight container in pot**

❷ **Position pump**

❸ **Place wire mesh over fountain outlet pipe**

❹ **Position drilled stone over pipe**

❺ **Add pebbles and plants**

barrel
pond

Bring the garden indoors by installing a large rustic barrel in a corner of the conservatory or sunroom, and converting it into a raised pond, complete with leafy backdrop and novelty waterspout.

This well-weathered specimen has been fitted with a rear shelf to support a fine backdrop of houseplants, that also acts as a perch for a whimsical waterspout. Easy to fit and spray-painted a neutral gray, the shelf is rendered virtually invisible once the pots of plants are in place. The houseplants themselves have been carefully chosen for their variety of foliage shape and their ability to soften the edges of the barrel, with arrangements of pebbles to fill in the gaps and add new textures. Spiky plants and beautiful flowers on long stems add height at the rear, with creeping, trailing varieties like ivy spilling over the sides in the foreground. This lush arrangement is also useful for concealing essential pipe work and cables. In contrast to the tangle of greenery behind, the water in the main part of the barrel is kept relatively free, in order to emphasize the gentle splash of the frog fountain.

You could drop a special basket into the barrel to contain your plants. Line it with burlap or a proprietary liner to prevent the soil from washing into the water.

▲ ❶ An electrical submersible pump needs to be concealed within the barrel, with the cable running up behind the shelf to feed the fountain ornament. It is better to overestimate the capacity pump you need when choosing a pump, if the feature is to be running continuously for any length of time.

▲ ❷ Wooden barrels create a rustic atmosphere and will set the tone for your indoor water feature. Used barrels will need to be checked to ensure that they are watertight and sealed or lined if necessary, but they do have a lot of character.

▲ ❸ Pebbles are great for filling the gaps between plants and features to create a natural effect and look particularly good beside water. You can buy them ready-washed in a range of types and sizes.

▲ **❶** Artillery plant, *Pilea microphylla*, has dense feathery foliage and originates in Central America. It thrives in most conditions, although it does have to be protected from frost, and can be propagated from half-inch (1.2cm) cuttings for planting in a bonsai arrangement.

miniature mountain
waterfall

ADVANTAGES

● Bonsai landscapes take up very little space.

● A fascinating hobby for all ages.

● Perfect for an oriental-inspired interior.

The same elements can be combined in an infinite variety of ways to create different effects.

The ancient Japanese art of bonsai—the pruning and wiring of trees and plants to miniaturize them—has developed over centuries, primarily to show off the gardener's skill. Today, these scaled-down landscapes make a delightful tabletop feature for homes too small to enjoy full-size specimens in the garden, and combined with rock and water as here, create the perfect blend of yang and yin according to Japanese and Chinese principles of harmony.

The rocks represent mountains populated by forests of artillery plant and juniper, through which water flows down into a calm pool populated by colorful goldfish. In this creation designed by Su Chin, the impression of perspective has been cleverly achieved by using a small clay Shiwan figure of a fisherman in the foreground, complete with fish on line, set beside the artificially gnarled trunk of the junipers, and the feathery foliage of the artillery looks like distant trees in the background. Areas of moss and liverwort provide the "ground cover" planting and soften the cement and fiberglass construction of the base.

▲ **❷** Shimpaku juniper, *Juniperus chinensis*, is a popular bonsai plant, the trunks and branches usually wired into weather-beaten shapes. Only the second year's woody growth is pruned: the needle foliage should be plucked rather than pinched out.

▼ **❸** Here, an ordinary terra-cotta tray has been used, painted gray to match the scenery.

THE CAST OF CHARACTERS

▼ **4** Chinese Shiwan figures are sculpted in clay and used to add a human touch and color to a bonsai landscape. This Yu Fu Fisherman with Fish gives the rocks and plants a new perspective and hints at other fish under the rocks.

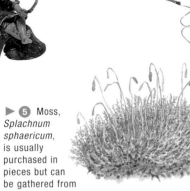

◀ **6** Liverwort, *Lunularia cruciata*, spreads well in damp places and will help hold the planting medium together.

▶ Goldfish will tolerate shallower conditions, so they are useful for adding real life and movement to a small water landscape. The moving water feature provides valuable oxygen, the rocks make welcome shelter.

▼ **9** When choosing river rocks, you need to decide whether they are going to be structural within the setting or merely ornamental. Scale and craggy character will all determine your choice. Use only washed stone and rock to avoid polluting the water.

▼ **7** Japanese mound juniper, *Juniperus chinensis procumbens* 'Nana', will grow into a representation of small trees in a bonsai setting. A collection of rooted cuttings is usually arranged on a piece of slate to develop a good root run before they are transferred to a rock position.

◀ **8** Japanese sweetflag, *Acorus gramineus*, is a cultivated bog grass available from aquarium stores. It likes cool, damp conditions and semi-shade, where it creates fan-shaped tufts about a third of their usual size in shallow soil.

▶ **5** Moss, *Splachnum sphaericum*, is usually purchased in pieces but can be gathered from the garden in spring and stored in a cool place between layers of newspaper until used. The soil beneath moss is porous and nutritious, so it makes a good base for other plants.

SETTING THE SCENE

BONSAI PLANTS
Roots and shoots are clipped and branches wired to maintain the miniature effect of trees and shrubs in bonsai. There are standard techniques and classical shapes such as the S shapes seen here, or "cloud pads" and "steps to heaven." Older plants have a fully mature look and will blossom, or leaves color and fall, according to season. You can buy specimens ready trained for creating a more complex landscape, or if you have the patience, learn the techniques to create your own. If you are using miniaturized outdoor plants, the garden must be kept outdoors for them to thrive and be brought indoors only occasionally as a special feature.

WATER
Moving water represents positive energy (qi) with the still pool below providing a calming influence. You will need an electric pump with an adjustable flow control small enough to be submerged in your container.

ROCK
Rock and stone are used to represent mountains and river boulders and are either specially constructed from modeling materials as described, or specially selected for their character, size, and shape, so any interesting cracks or fissures are important. Rock needs positioning where it will be viewed to best advantage; you also need to make sure it is not too obscured by plant growth.

TRAY
The style and size of the tray is important, and a wide range of shallow glazed ceramic bowls and dishes are available specifically for bonsai, mostly in shades of gray, green, and blue to complement the landscape. These might be square, rectangular, or circular in shape; some have small feet to raise them slightly. However, any container might be used, providing it is waterproof and of the correct dimensions.

BEHIND THE SCENES

A BONSAI LANDSCAPE

The tray needs to be waterproof and deep enough for the water pump to be completely submerged. This one was specially painted to blend with the landscape. Height is provided by modeling contours out of chicken wire and cement fondue, which is flexible and lightweight.

1 Mold the structural base with fine-gauge chicken wire to create the contours of the rocks and mountain required. Run the tubing through the base to the waterfall outflow at the top left-hand corner. Cover the base with fiberglass, available in small sheets from craft and modeling stores.

2 Model the bulk of the waterfall and other contours using cement fondue, which is strong and weather-resistant, and allow to harden. Paint it onto the fiberglass with a brush and build up the levels in stages like papier-mâché. Cover with wet newspaper and a damp cloth, then leave to dry for one day.

3 Line the water tray area with thick plastic, and position the pump where it will not be seen. Connect the tubing to the pump.

4 Add the water and test the effect of the waterfall. When you are satisfied, you can complete the planting. Use the good, porous soil from under your moss pieces, and mix it with a little sand and loam until it can be molded into a kind of sausage that will encourage plants to root without slipping into the water.

Japanese sweetflag, *Acorus gramineus*

1 Create the base with chicken wire and fiberglass

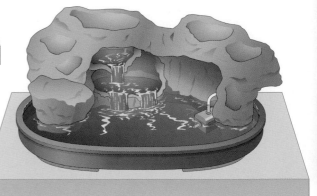

2 Add contours with cement and then paint

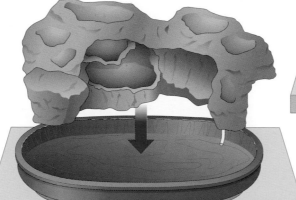

3 Position base on tray

4 Add pump and test water

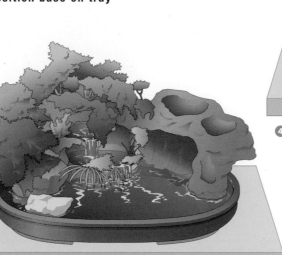

5 Plant the foliage

POINTS TO REMEMBER

● Make a model of the contours of the garden in modeling dough or clay to get the shape and scale right before tackling the chicken wire and cement fondue of the real structure.

● Moss will grow anywhere, even over the cement, so it is useful for disguising and softening hard features.

● Use rainwater, not tap water, to fill the pool and to water plants.

● Feed the fish floating pellets, not flakes, to avoid polluting the water.

Juniperus chinensis procumbens 'Nana'

▲ **1** You can buy pebbles by the bag from your local garden center, or make your own collection from the backyard, providing the stones are well washed before being introduced to water.

group of containers

▼ **2** A submersible pump is necessary to run the bubble fountain, but these can be bought small enough to tuck into the most modest of pools or reservoirs.

ADVANTAGES

● Decorative containers particularly suit indoor settings.

● Looks good all year round.

● Good variety of features in the minimum of space.

Glazed ceramic planters are often sold in matching nests of different sized bowls or urns that are ideal for planting up and positioning in stylish groups of three or five. The largest containers make great freestanding water gardens, possibly incorporating one of the smaller types of fountain, or maybe a few miniature aquatic plants. You can even add a few fish and a dwarf water lily if you are prepared to add a small electric filter.

This glossy blue trio combines three different yet complementary garden concepts within a single, close-knit arrangement: a moving water feature full of life and sound, the cool calm of a still pond, and an architectural arrangement of spiky plants and pebbles. The pebbles, collected on family trips to the beach, are a clever visual link between the pots and even spill onto the floor to soften the effect of the overall outline. The largest container is home to a tranquil pool complete with pond weed and colorful artificial water lily; its companion containers include a lively bubble feature and a lush fountainlike bromeliad.

For a more contemporary feel, use polished glass instead of pebbles, in colors chosen to complement the containers.

▲ Artificial flowers can look remarkably realistic, and need little care and maintenance. This silk water lily provides year-round interest in the pool and has been combined with real plants.

THE CAST OF CHARACTERS

Fairy moss, *Azolla caroliniana*, is an aquatic fern, perfect for indoor pools since it is not fully hardy outside. ◄ ❸

▼ Bromeliads, with their bold foliage and bright colors, are popular designer plants and can be guaranteed to put on a good display.

► ❺ If you don't like the idea of artificial flowers, dwarf water lilies, varieties of *Nymphaea pygmaea*, are perfect for smaller pools and container ponds, and come in a choice of beautiful bloom colors.

▼ Mother in Law's Tongue, *Sanseviera trifasciata*, makes a handsome clump of leathery swordlike leaves, and is a fine specimen plant in a modern setting.

▲ ❹ You can buy sets of planters in a good choice of designs and finishes. These glazed bowls have a strong Mediterranean feel, but could look equally good in an oriental setting.

► Ponytail plant, *Beaucarnia recurvata*, thrives in centrally heated rooms and produces a wild fountain of arching stems from the top of a stout woody stem.

▲ Boston fern, *Nephrolepis exaltata 'Bostoniensis,'* makes a good-sized clump of strong, deep-green, crested fronds, an excellent specimen plant for pots and hanging baskets.

SETTING THE SCENE

MATCHING CONTAINERS

For a stylish coordinated look, use containers of different sizes and shapes but in a matching color or finish. For example, a selection of pots, bowls, and urns in terra-cotta would have equal impact to these strong Mediterranean blues. Note that groups of odd numbers always look more pleasing than a more formal, even-numbered arrangement.

PEBBLES

This indoor garden display shows some of the excellent ways pebbles can be used as a decorative feature: on the floor, as a mulch around plants, and as an integral part of a water feature. Note how different-sized stones have been used for variety and to suit their location.

PLANTING

Planting here has been kept to a minimum for ease of maintenance, so specimens are chosen for impact. You could create a more lush leafy effect by adding foliage plants such as ferns and ivies in nearby containers.

BUBBLE FOUNTAIN

Bubble-action fountain spouts are ideal for smaller water features since they provide the sight and sound of moving water without too much splash. The water is recycled via a small pump in the receptacle below. Incorporating the fountain with other containers provides the opportunity to conceal the electrical cable.

BEHIND THE SCENES

A VARIETY OF CONTAINER GARDENS

A mix-and-match arrangement of coordinated containers offers endless scope for different miniature garden ideas. Here, a watery theme combines a still pool, a bubbling fountain, and a lush spiky plant in a bed of small stones.

❶ Ensure the two largest bowls are completely clean and dry, using a blow-dryer if necessary. Silicone a circular patch of liner to the base of both containers to cover the drainage holes.

❷ In the largest bowl, fill with water and, if using tap water, leave to stand for the chlorine to evaporate. Put in your choice of aquatic plants such as pondweed, which simply floats on the surface, and the silk or real water lilies.

❸ In the middle bowl, position the pump in the base and fit with a bubbler outlet. Cover with a wire mesh and fill the bowl with water.

❹ Top with pebbles and run the electrical cable to a nearby outlet. Turn on and adjust the flow.

❺ In the third container, fill the base with a layer of gravel or pebbles for drainage, and top with compost. Plant a suitably dramatic houseplant, and mulch with small stones or gravel.

Bromeliad

❶ **Silicone liner to base**

❷ **Add water and aquatic plants to largest bowl**

POINTS TO REMEMBER

● If your chosen containers are going to be used to hold water, make sure they are watertight by sealing any drainage holes. Alternatively, line with a slightly smaller, plastic pot.

● Position your feature near a window, so that there is plenty of light to highlight the water and to encourage plants to grow. Ponds in dark corners can have a dark, dank feel to them.

● Place your pots on a raised plinth if you want to give the feature greater prominence.

❸ **Fit pump, add mesh and water to middle bowl**

❹ **Top with pebbles**

❺ **Add pebbles and plant to smallest bowl**

mosaic *table*

▲ **1** Mosaic is supplied as small tiles that have to be cemented in place to create the pattern of your choice. It can also be purchased as strips or sheets in ready-made designs. An individual alternative would be to create a crazy paving effect with pieces of broken china.

If you do not have the time or skills to make a table, simply cover an old table in mosaic tiles, and float candles in a bowl.

In this colorful mosaic design, a miniature pond and planting recess have been cleverly incorporated into a low table to combine a water feature, a work of art, and an item of furniture in a single unit. It is handsome enough to grace the smartest living room, where it would make a stunning conversation piece with little risk of spillage from soil or water.

The table is simply made from medium-density fiberboard with intersecting compartments built in for the sunken features. These can be easily adapted to your own ideas and might include a larger planting trough or even a small fountain feature. The basic table is quickly transformed into something more decorative and highly individual by the application of bright mosaic tiles and colored grouting. To maintain the modern art look, this table has been planted with sculptural cacti, a multi-branched Tree Opuntia straight out of a cowboy movie, and a pin cushion Tom Thumb cactus. Other floor-standing potted plants can be used to soften the outline of the table: here a bushy oregano plant is a good contrast to cacti and candles. By day, the tiny pond is decorated with petals and blooms from the garden; at night floating candles highlight the water and bring a luminous glow to the ceramic tiles.

▲ **2** Floating candles are a beautiful way to highlight a water feature after dark and are available in many scents and colors. They are even available sculpted to look like water lilies.

▶ **3** Tree Opuntia, *O. brasiliensis*, produces spiny angular pads which grow into a treelike shape off a basal section. It is a desert cactus from the warm semi-desert regions of the United States.

THE CAST OF CHARACTERS

▶ **4** Red hooked spines and a scarlet central flower are features of the dumpy Tom Thumb Cactus, *Parodia sanguinicola*, that is easily propagated from cuttings.

▶ Polka Dot Plant, *Hypoestes phyllostachya*, is ideal for modern interiors and fun schemes with its dark-green, pale-pink, spotted foliage. Plants look good grouped in sunken containers and troughs.

▼ Emerald fern, *Asparagus densiflorus*, has delicate fernlike stems perfect for softening the outline of features or contrasting with other, fleshy foliage species.

◀ **5** Oregano, *Origanum*, is an aromatic herb that grows into a fresh green bushy plant. In summer it produces attractive spikes of purple flowers.

▲ The easy to grow Spider Plant, *Chlorophytum comosum*, makes a lush, arching fountain of striped foliage and long stems of tiny flowers and little plantlets.

◀ Silver crown, *Cotyledon undulata*, is distinguished by its stems of strange fleshy, fan-shaped leaves with a soft silver appearance. It looks particularly good in massed groups, that show off the foliage to best advantage.

▶ Urn plant, *Aechmea fasciata*, is an exciting looking plant that makes a large rosette of leathery, finely patterned leaves from which an exotic bloom rises after three to four years.

SETTING THE SCENE

TABLE WITH SUNKEN POOL
Building your own furniture offers wonderful scope to be really creative. Recessed troughs and built-in compartments in a table can be designed to house your favorite accessories and features. You can paint, stain, or tile the table in your choice of finish to suit your decorative scheme.

MOSAIC
Mosaic tiles are available in kit form or individual strips for creating your own effects, from craft stores and specialist art stockists. Buy in single colors to blend your own design combinations, or work with a ready-made collection of complementary shades. A colored tint in the grouting is a stylish finishing touch.

CACTI
Unusual and ornamental, cacti come in many wacky shapes and forms, and if you give them the right treatment, about half the cactus varieties grown indoors will even produce exotic flowers within three to four years.

CANDLES
Candles and water are a lovely combination after dark and the floating type are perfect for adding to indoor pools—especially if you are planning a dinner party. Colors can be chosen to match your dinner service or your carpet; many are scented and claim to have therapeutic effects.

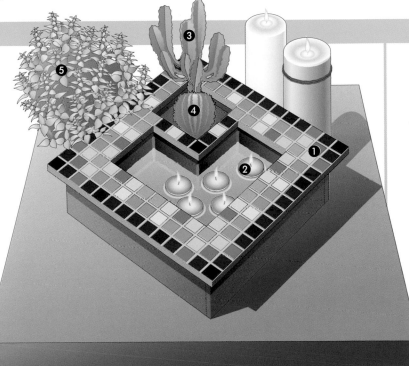

BEHIND THE SCENES

MOSAIC TABLE WITH POOL AND PLANTS

The table can be built to any size you wish, providing it is well supported. A larger pool might support a small collection of aquatic plants and even fish, if you installed a suitable filter system (in which case you should design the table so that the cables can exit out of sight). The finished look will be as bold or subtle as the mosaic tiles you choose.

1 Construct a shallow boxlike tabletop from medium-density fiberboard, building in a network of compartments for plants and water.

2 Line the section that will hold water with flexible pond liner; staple it in place and trim.

3 Use mosaic tiles to create a colorful pattern around the top of the table and stick it into place with the recommended adhesive.

4 Grout between the tiles with a waterproof grout, tinted to complement the color of the tiles.

5 Fill the planting section with soil and add water to the mini pool. Add plants and candles both inside and outside the feature.

1 Construct boxlike table top

2 Line the water-holding section

3 Decorate top with mosaic tiles

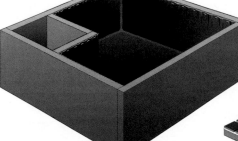

4 Grout between the tiles

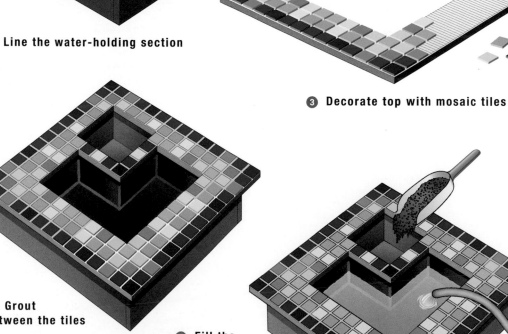

5 Fill the water and plant sections

POINTS TO REMEMBER

● When creating an original mosaic design, it is a good idea to plan it out first on graph paper and color it in with pens or pencils to check the effect from different angles. If you do this to scale, it will be a help when ordering the tiles.

● A series of recessed compartments will look more stylish if you restrict yourself to geometric shapes, and visually overlap or intersect them.

● Instead of candles, use spotlights and uplighters near the table to create interesting effects after dark.

▲ **①** Underwater lighting is available as single or multiple spotlights, depending on the size of the pond and the effect you are trying to achieve. Alternatively, use room spotlights to produce lighted reflections from highlighted poolside features such as plants and ornaments.

② The timber surrounding this raised pond has been stained a cool blue. You can choose one of many interesting shades available as stains and varnishes for adding character to garden features.

Using a raised pond as an indoor feature gives it greater effect and may be safer and more convenient than a sunken one if there are children or wheelchair users in the household.

mobile mini flower *pond*

This miniature square pond looks good by day or night with its all-around border of brightly colored plants and underwater lighting. Optional castors allow for easy transport to different sites, or—without wheels— the pond would look good on a large tabletop.

The blue-stained timber of the surround sets the scene for a colorful combination of foliage and flowering plants, which blends the harlequin leaves of coleus and begonias with the massed blooms of pretty lobelia and impatiens. Although the pond is small, the planting includes a good variety of leaf shapes too, from spiky festuca and fleshy hostas, to the delicate spreading fronds of creeping jenny. Many of the plants are pot-grown annuals, so they can be easily replaced as required to keep the feature looking good whatever the season. Any gaps between the plants are filled with smooth, bluish pebbles, the perfect link between the water and timber. Even the water in the pond has been populated with lush water lettuce and slender rushes to contribute to the overall display.

ADVANTAGES

- Colorful display can be simply updated seasonally.

- Castors enable the display to be moved around to suit changes in interior décor and to catch maximum light.

- After-dark interest.

Castors make heavy, raised features easier to move.

◄ **③** *Juncus effusus* 'Vittatus' is a golden variegated form of the soft rush suitable for smaller ponds. Remove any plain green stems to keep the stripes.

► **④** The painted nettle, *Coleus blumei,* is usually grown as an annual and offers a wide variety of patterned foliage in strong shades of red, bronze, cream, and purple.

▼ **⑤** *Ajuga,* or bugle, makes good ground cover with its dark blue, pink, or purple mintlike foliage, and will tolerate a shady position.

THE CAST OF CHARACTERS

▼ **6** Hostas are excellent pondside foliage plants with their lush, pleated leaves and tall stems of early summer flowers. There are many forms, such as blues, grays, golds, stripes, and patterns.

◄ Begonias are native to moist tropical and subtropical regions and many are grown as indoor plants. Some are prized for their bright, glossy blooms, but others produce striking textured and colored foliage.

► *Impatiens* or Busy Lizzie plants are widely grown as indoor and patio plants where they can offer an ever increasing range of colors and a free-flowering habit. They will grow in sun or light shade.

▼ **7** Lobelia has many forms, including this pretty pink-flowered plant popular for summer bedding schemes, hanging baskets, and window boxes.

◄ **8** *Festuca*, or fescue, is a useful tufted grass, particularly the mound-forming varieties, which are available in a choice of spiky shades, including blue.

▲ Edging lobelia, *L. erinus*, often has a semi-trailing habit frequently used to edge summer bedding schemes and hanging baskets. Given a moist soil in sun or shade, it will make a mass of tiny blue, purple, maroon, or lilac flowers according to variety.

▼ *Lysimachia nummularia* 'Aurea' or golden creeping Jenny (moneywort) is frequently seen beside ponds or streams where it spreads freely to make a carpet of tiny pale yellow-green leaves.

▲ **9** *Houttuynia* makes good ground cover beside ponds or in damp areas with its quickly spreading heart-shaped leaves. *H. cordata* 'Chameleon' (syn 'Tricolor', 'Variegata') is especially striking with its red, cream, pink, and green variegation.

► **10** The water lettuce, *Pistia stratiotes*, is a tender floating aquatic with fleshy green leaves. It is easy to propagate from the clusters of young plants that grow out from the main plant.

SETTING THE SCENE

SMALL RAISED POND
Lack of size need not mean lack of effect with an indoor pond if you choose a strong geometric preformed shape and highlight it with a colorful surrounding display of plants and features.

PLANTING
Be bold in your choice of pondside planting with brightly patterned foliage and colorful seasonal flowers to create stunning contrasts of shape and color. Keeping the plants in pots hidden in compost behind a timber edge, like an outsize window box, means they can be replaced easily when past their best.

TIMBER EDGING
A timber edge used to conceal the liner of a raised pond is inexpensive and easy to install, but also offers many creative options such as stains and paints to add color and texture to your feature.

LIGHTING
Low-voltage underwater spotlights will light up a pond in a dark corner, or one sited in an area used primarily in the evenings. Color filters are also available that will enable you to change the effect should you wish to.

BEHIND THE SCENES

RAISED PLANTED POND

Freestanding, preformed ponds and other suitable containers are available in a selection of shapes and sizes suitable for creating indoor features. The receptacles themselves usually need disguising with some kind of surround such as the timber used here. You may decide to add wheels so that you can reposition the pond with ease.

❶ Buy or build a timber box from sawn and sanded lumber at least 6 inches (15cm) wider around than the perimeter of your proposed pond. Add castors for additional mobility.

❷ Line the base with heavy-duty PVC or butyl pond liner. Trim so that it is not visible from the top, and tack into place on the inside where it cannot be seen. Position the preformed pond in the construction, off-center.

❸ Stain or paint the outside of the timber the color of your choice.

❹ Put in a 4-inch (10cm) layer of pebbles or small stones in the bottom between the timber and the pool. Fill it to the rim with high-quality compost.

❺ Position plants directly into the compost, or insert plant pots up to the rim and fill any gaps between them with smooth stones or pebbles.

❻ Fill slowly with water using a hose. Place your chosen underwater spotlights into the base of the pond and run the cable to a nearby socket. You may need a brick or plinth to get them to the right height.

Water lettuce, *Pistia stratiotes*

❶ **Add castors to timber box**

❷ **Line base and add preformed pond**

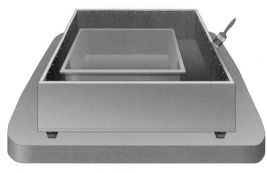
❸ **Stain or paint the box**

❹ **Add pebbles and compost**

❺ **Position plants and pebbles**

❻ **Fill pond with water**

POINTS TO REMEMBER

● Look for extra-large rigid containers such as giant plastic planters or wide troughs that could be used as your pond liner.

● Check that you have a suitable electrical socket nearby if you are planning to include lighting or a fountain in the pond.

● Pond, plants, and water add up to quite a weight, so if your pond is being installed on a suspended floor, make sure that the floor joists are sound and strong enough to support it.

● If your chosen pond liner is not of rigid construction, you will have to position it on a bed of sand supported by a timber framework (see page 98).

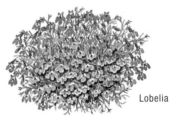

Lobelia

oriental water
garden

▲ **1** You can buy bags of ready-washed pebbles in a choice of colors and sizes. They are ideal for pebble pools and bubble fountains, as the watert enhances their subtle variations in color and markings.

The Japanese *shishi odoshi*, or deer scarer, is a traditional oriental water feature that once served a strictly practical purpose keeping wild animals away from prized plants. Lengths of hollow bamboo are cleverly tied together to form a water-powered pivot, one piece trickling into another until the weight of the water overbalances it and the bamboo drops onto a strategically placed stone with a regular "dock" sound.

▲ **2** Bamboo is available in different sizes and lengths for creating your own trims and features. If you plan to use it for water features, it should be waterproofed to prevent it from splitting.

Here, the spout feature has been set among a stylish bamboo-edged bed of pebbles, the sump concealed beneath a smoothly elegant slate slab. Positioned on the stone-tiled floor of a conservatory, the contrasts are subtle, a harmony of pink and lilac grays that help create a visual sense of peace, as well as providing the soothing sound of moving water. The smart, clean lines of this feature have given a time-honored water feature a fresh, contemporary feel, enhanced by the fact that the slate edging has a generous overlap which completely hides the pump and water reservoir to give the impression that the whole feature is floating above the floor. To maintain that important minimalist feel, the fountain is decorated with a handful of seasonal petals, but planting is restricted to nearby containers.

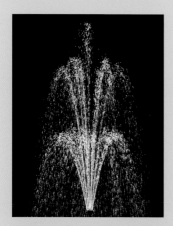

Larger raised pebble ponds might benefit from the different effect of a tiered plume spray.

▼ **3** Stone, slate, or marble-effect floor tiles are tough enough for a conservatory or patio, yet smart enough for an interior finish.

THE CAST OF CHARACTERS

◄ ❹ Scented geraniums, *Pelargonium*, add sweet and spicy scents, as well as pretty flowers and foliage to a planting scheme. Pinch the leaves on passing to release the aroma of roses, cloves, or lemon.

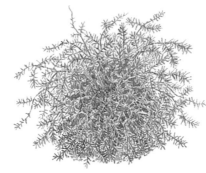

▲ The emerald fern, *Asparagus densiflorus*, has arching fernlike fronds of delicate foliage that is ideal for softening the background to smaller water features.

► Lemon geranium, *Pelargonium crispum 'Variegatum'*, grows into an attractive bush of aromatic small leaves in shades of pale green and cream with wavy edges.

◄ Club moss, *Selaginella martensii*, is a creeping plant that soon creates a dense mat of greenery, perfect for all-green oriental schemes.

▼ Flowering *Hibiscus calphyllus* is a tropical flowering shrub, the bright yellow flowers distinguished by a purple-brown eye.

► The miniature iris, *Iris reticulata*, makes a beautiful scaled-down display of sweet-scented iris blooms in shades of blue and mauve with yellow markings.

► Maples are a Japanese classic; for indoor gardens, the flowering maple *Abutilon hybridum* features the familiar maple-shaped leaves, but also attractive flowers of red, pink, yellow, or white. There is even a variegated form, *A. pictum 'Thompsonii'*.

SETTING THE SCENE

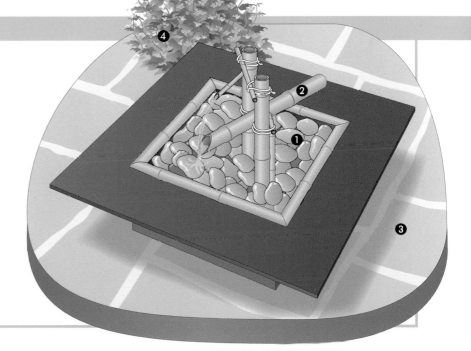

BAMBOO FOUNTAIN
Quick and easy to install, the *shishi odoshi* is clean-looking but curvaceous, the perfect small-scale moving water feature for homes adopting an oriental or modern decorative style. The rhythmic sound can be as relaxing as a slow ticking long-case clock in the right setting.

PEBBLE POOL
Pebble ponds with their concealed reservoir of water make good non-splash indoor features, but this one is extra stylish with its strictly square shape and sophisticated tabletop surround.

SLATE SURROUND
Smooth, shiny slate is a fine natural material with a textural appearance and a contemporary feel that looks particularly good in conjunction with water.

STONE FLOOR TILES
Good-looking stone or quarry tiles underfoot are hardwearing and waterproof, an excellent choice for linking both outdoor and indoor areas.

BEHIND THE SCENES

BAMBOO SPOUT IN A PEBBLE POND

A small, submersible pump will be sufficient to recycle the water through the bamboo from a small hidden reservoir below the bamboo spout. It must be run quietly so as not to spoil the restful effect of the feature, and have sufficient headroom to operate efficiently within the sump.

1 Build the water reservoir from medium-density fiberboard. Line with a piece of flexible liner and place the pump into position. Cover with a wire mesh.

2 Fit over a wide rim, made from spray-painted fiberboard or a cut slate tile, tucking the liner underneath for a neat finish. Split some pieces of bamboo with an axe and hammer to produce the trim, and glue into place with silicone to make a watertight seal.

3 Use a section of broom handle and a hammer to knock out the notches in the center of the bamboo you are using for the spout, leaving the bottom section so that the water cannot go all the way through. Cut one end at an angle, then drill a hole in the center, and insert a piece of dowel or smaller piece of bamboo to act as a pivot.

4 For the upright sections, make a firm base from a piece of wood and insert two pieces of bamboo to make the support. In one, you will need to knock out all the notches bar the bottom section and insert a piece of pipe into a drilled hole, sealing it with silicone. Drill a second hole further up the bamboo and insert the smaller piece of bamboo that will feed the spout, using silicone to make watertight. Seal the top of the bamboo with a piece of knocked out section and silicone.

5 Tie all the sections of bamboo together using string or twine and place it in position, connecting the supply pipe to the pump. Fill the sump with water; check the flow and adjust until the spout is operating correctly. Top with pebbles to finish.

Pelargonium crispum 'Variegatum'

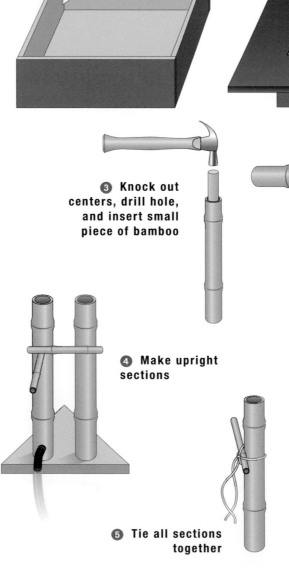

1 Build the water reservoir

2 Fit the wide rim

3 Knock out centers, drill hole, and insert small piece of bamboo

4 Make upright sections

5 Tie all sections together

POINTS TO REMEMBER

● The regular clack of a *shishi odoshi* is not to everyone's taste and can appear more irritating than relaxing to some ears. Check one out at your local garden center to see how compatible you are; there are other styles of bamboo spout if you like the look but not the sound effect.

● To prevent bamboo pipes from splitting, knock out the nodal dividers inside with a metal rod and insert a piece of garden hose.

● As an alternative to string for binding the bamboo poles together, you could use strong black wool yarn, copper wire, or red ribbon.

decorative wall
spout

▼ **1** You can buy decorative trellis arches in a wide choice of ready-made shapes and designs. Stain or paint to create different effects. Alternatively, reconstituted stone arches can be supplied in sections for fastening to the wall.

▶ **2** Wall-mounted water features like this spout and classic shell basin are great space savers for smaller homes and gardens that don't have room for a full-scale water garden. It offers the chance to enjoy the sight and sound of moving water, plus a small selection of pond plants, in an area of wall space no bigger than a small dresser.

ADVANTAGES

● A simple wall spout has been extended into a much more imposing feature by setting it within a trellis arch, with a large semi formal pond below. The cascade of water and vertical planting help to link all these elements together and make them look as one.

● With everything well contained, this is an easy-to-maintain water garden for a conservatory or entrance hall.

● Looks good even when the pump is turned off.

● Suitable for children and wheelchair users.

A decorative wall fountain, redolent of a more leisurely, ornamental age, makes a superb focal point in the home, both from its visual impact and the refreshing sound of the splash of moving water. Surrounding planting is usually kept fairly minimal: just enough to soften the outline without hiding the main feature.

This old-fashioned lead water spout, in the shape of a ram's head, has been positioned against a plain white, rough-rendered wall for maximum light and effect. The water spills from the head into a classic wall-mounted shell basin, then into a semi-circular raised pool below which has been built in brick and painted white to match the walls. The tumbling water is the main focus of attention, but splashes of color are provided by a few carefully selected plants—pondside primulas and variegated iris planted in the water stand sentinel on either side of the spout; and bright pink pelargoniums make a splash of long-lasting color around the base. The spout itself has been made into a much larger feature by setting it within a handsome trellis arch entwined with convolvulus, (morning glory vine) and pretty clematis.

◀ **3** There are more than 200 varieties of clematis, with their mass of showy flowers and, later, fluffy seed heads. They are excellent and speedy climbers providing the roots are well shaded in well-drained soil and the flowers receive plenty of sun.

THE CAST OF CHARACTERS

▼ **4** *Convolvulus sabatius*, the morning glory vine, is a delicate but prolific trailing perennial that makes a curtain of foliage and lilac-blue flowers. It grows best over walls or in hanging baskets.

◄ **6** With their bold sword-shaped foliage and bright, exotic blooms, iris are a water garden must for many pond owners. This variegated yellow-striped variety is the perfect link between pond and spout and looks decorative even when not in flower.

▼ **9** *Pelargoniums* can always be relied on for providing flashes of brilliant color right through the summer months.

► **7** Primula are closely associated with pond and stream edges and generally prefer a shady position. There are around 400 species to choose from, satisfying a wide range of positions and with a huge variety of flower size, color, and shape.

▲ **8** *Hardenbergia*, or pea vine, is a twining climber that makes exotic clusters of white-eyed purple flowers.They prefer a moist, lime-free soil and will grow in full sun or shade.

10 Like the wall in the background, the brick-edged pond has been painted white to maintain a light, bright feel against which the darkness of the wall spout and brilliance of the flowers can be thrown into relief.

► **5** To produce a more suitable background for the wall spout, the wall has been rough-rendered and painted white. This adds light and texture, yet remains neutral enough to set off elaborate features and colorful plants to their best advantage.

SETTING THE SCENE

WALL SPOUT
Whether a lead ram's head, a stone lion, or a spouting dolphin, the old classical designs are still favored for adding a real touch of class and tradition to the home. A heavy artifact like this needs firm fixing, so make sure the wall is up to it and that you use the strongest screws and wall plugs.

SEMI-FORMAL POND
Building your own pond means it can be any size or shape you wish. Pleasingly, this semi-circular style reflects the shape of the arch above and is slightly larger than required, so it can be used to grow a small selection of interesting marginal plants too.

TRELLIS
A ready-made trellis arch simply screwed to the wall puts the wall spout into a more elaborate setting and makes a larger feature of it. It also provides the means to train flowering climbers up the wall, creating a delightful arbor effect.

PLANTING
To enhance such a decorative feature, a limited selection of colorful plants were chosen: golden variegated iris, hot pink pelargoniums, free-blooming clematis, pea vine, and convolvulus, as pretty as any wallpaper or furnishing fabric in this interior setting.

BEHIND THE SCENES

WALL SPOUT AND POND

A spout and pond may be economical on wall space, but its position requires careful consideration as it would not be an easy job to move it once installed. You need to decide where it will have most impact—especially if the feature can be viewed from several angles—or where you will be able to sit and enjoy it. Turn to page 16 for extra guidance on building the base pond.

❶ Sand and paint the wall behind. When dry, mark where the spout and bowl will be positioned and drill the holes for the screws: get someone to hold the features up for you to choose the best position if necessary, and use a plumb line to get them aligned correctly. Screw the spout and bowl firmly to the wall, using strong screws and wall plugs.

POINTS TO REMEMBER

● You must build the pond all around, including the rear wall, to ensure that it is watertight. Do not try to butt your construction onto the existing wall.

● Wider coping can be fitted around the top of the pond to create a seating area.

● Adjust the cascade so that it does not splash beyond the confines of the pond or you will need to refill the feature with water regularly.

● You can buy ready-made semi-circular base ponds in concrete or fiberglass which can simply be pushed against the wall and painted to suit.

---

❷ There should be a channel in the back of the ram's head to accommodate the hose. If not, you will have to chisel one into the wall. Clip the hose to the wall using plumber's pipe fasteners. The pipe can be painted to match the wall to disguise it, or concealed behind plant foliage.

❸ Start building the base pond, making sure it is central to the wall spout. On a firm concrete base, use bricks and mortar to build up a raised semi-circular shape. To draw the shape initially, fasten a string to a center point on the wall behind and use a pencil or piece of chalk on the other end to scribe a semi circle.

❹ When the mortar has hardened, line the pond loosely with a piece of black flexible liner and fill slowly with a hose, adjusting the liner as it is pulled into shape.

❺ Mortar coping stones along the top edge of the pond to hide the top of the liner, continuing it along the back wall as a ledge. Paint bricks white to match the rear wall. Attach the pump in the pond to the hose and plug into a safe electrical outlet nearby.

❻ Screw the trellis to the wall behind the wall spout, and add the dish.

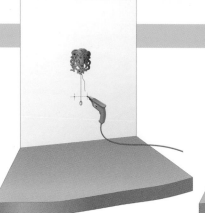

❶ Drill holes

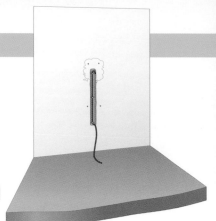

❷ Clip hose to wall

❸ Add head and build base pond

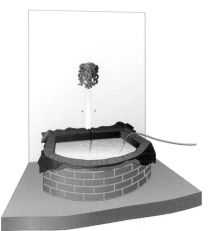

❹ Line pond and slowly fill with water

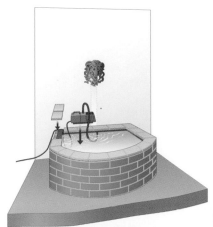

❺ Insert pump and add coping stones

❻ Screw trellis to wall and add dish

meditation
corner

▲ ▶ **1** Gravel and pebbles are available in a wide choice of colors and sizes to suit the effect you are aiming to achieve. An area of smooth pebbles combined with raked sand, for example, would create a more oriental atmosphere. Or you could purchase colorful chips of glass or aquarium stones for a more contemporary effect.

ADVANTAGES

● A combination of natural materials is a good antidote to interior ornaments and soft furnishings.

● Limiting the planting to bold foliage plants has a restful effect.

● Concrete construction for the pond offers complete flexibility of shape and size.

● Blinds and large plants do a good job of filtering strong sunlight.

The lush green of handsome foliage plants and the tranquility of water are well known to have a soothing, therapeutic effect. So what better decorative feature to incorporate into a corner of the living room or conservatory than this oasislike meditation area, complete with pool and exotic planting?

This relatively small area can then be transformed into a pleasing combination of natural materials—a tiny but craggy pool and cascade resting on a bed of pea shingle, and a dramatic display of foliage plants providing interest at every level, whether seated or standing. Glossy ficus, Schleffera and Monstera, the Swiss cheese plant, do much to raise the eyes—and spirit—upward and make a leafy backdrop, whereas pretty maidenhair fern and the striking white-veined goosefoot plant (*Syngonium*) soften the contours of the pool below. The colorful markings of *Caladium bicolor* (angel's wings) and spiky *Dracæna* add further color and interest without the need for showy flowers. Keeping the effect simple is the key to tranquility—even the floor has been given over to a tactile but visually undemanding carpet of sand and small stones that laps out from the pool like soothing waves.

▲ **2** Ficus is an excellent plant for the back of larger plant displays with plenty of handsome foliage shapes to choose from: *Ficus bennendijkii* looks like an evergreen weeping willow; *Ficus benjamina*, the weeping fig, is a popular houseplant with its curtain of small pointed leaves on arching branches; *Ficus elastica* is a dramatic rubber plant sporting large, glossy, dark-green leaves on a strong stem up to 10 feet (3m) high.

THE CAST OF CHARACTERS

◀ *Shleffera arboricola* is a tall plant displaying handsome hand-shaped leaves. There are various forms, including the easy-to-grow 'Compacta', that make a dense tower of distinctive foliage said to absorb pollutants from the air.

▶ **③** *Caladium bicolor*, or angel's wings, has brilliant red and green patterned, heart-shaped leaves that enjoy a bright, humid atmosphere out of direct sunlight.

▼ The popular giant Swiss cheese plant, *Monstera deliciosa*, originates in the South American rain forests and makes a huge plant of outsize, glossy leaves with distinctive slashes. It grows best around a mossy pole that can be kept damp at all times.

▶ *Dracæna fragrans* is a striking upright plant with bold spiky foliage. There are various forms, including those with slender spikes and broader strap-shaped leaves, as well as red coloring.

▼ **④** The goosefoot plant *Syngonium podophyllum* 'Imperial White' has beautifully marked, heart-shaped leaves and can be grown as a climber up to 6 feet (1.8m) or more. Prune the climbing stems if you want a bushier plant.

▶ *Cordyline australis*, or New Zealand cabbage tree, is a splendid architectural plant making a large fountain of swordlike foliage. There are various forms featuring different red/green/yellow combinations.

▼ *Fatsia japonica*, the Japanese *aralia*, with its large, glossy hand-shaped leaves, is a handsome plant that prefers cooler conditions.

▶ *Philodendron scandens*, the sweetheart plant, Is an excellent and vigorous climber with its tumbling mass of glossy heart-shaped leaves. It is best grown in a hanging basket or up a mossy pole.

◀ *Dieffenbachia*, the dumb cane, is grown for its handsome green and yellow mottled leaves, but the sap is poisonous, so it needs careful handling.

▶ **⑤** *Epipremnum*, or devil's ivy, is a fine climbing or trailing plant with bright green or splendidly marbled heart-shaped foliage, according to variety.

SETTING THE SCENE

WINDOW BLINDS
Blinds are essential for screening large windows from strong summer sunshine. These neutral horizontal blinds are a good contrast to the vertical stems and foliage of surrounding plants, but adjustable slatted blinds in natural wood, canvas roller blinds, or even diaphanous muslin curtains, would do the job equally well.

GRAVEL AND SHINGLE
Natural materials underfoot such as sand, pebbles, or gravel are perfectly in tune with the meditative nature of this feature and encourage the plants to look more in keeping with this setting.

DRAMATIC FOLIAGE DISPLAY
Plants provide an interesting variety of foliage shapes and colors, from deeply veined *Caladium* and *Syngonium* to spiky *Dracaenas* and giant glossy *Monstera*, so there is no need for bright flowers to disturb the tranquility of this corner.

POOL
This semi-formal circular pool, relatively uncrowded by plants or other features, makes an excellent focal point among the bold foliage. For a slightly more formal effect, a raised circular or oval pool faced in stone and softened by ferns or similar greenery, would work equally well.

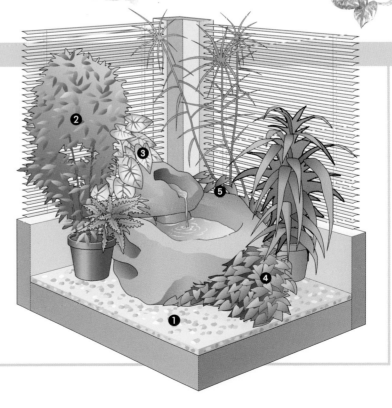

BEHIND THE SCENES

CRAGGY POOL AND CASCADE

A coat of concrete will transform mundane, modern-looking plastic or fiberglass into something far more in keeping with a natural setting. Here, a premolded pool and miniature cascade—available in a wide range of shapes and sizes from aquatic centers—has been given a more sympathetic feel.

1 Put the molded pool in its final position, angling it into the corner and allowing space behind for access to plants.

2 Paint all over the outside with a 5 percent solution of PVA or craft glue and water. Allow to dry.

3 Start applying coats of 4:1 stiff concrete mix to which you have added waterproofer and coloring according to the manufacturer's instructions. Allow to harden completely between coats.

4 Build up the layers for a rough, craggy look. When satisfied with the final appearance, fill with water and soften the outline with surrounding plants.

Caladium bicolor

1 Place molded pool in final position

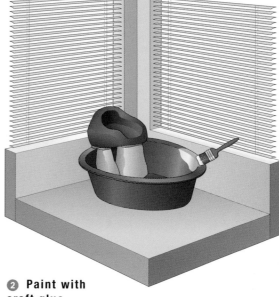

2 Paint with craft glue

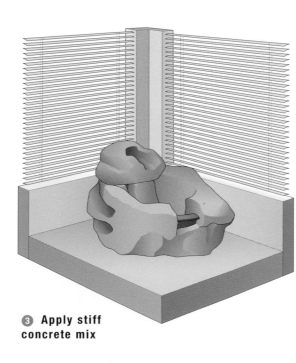

3 Apply stiff concrete mix

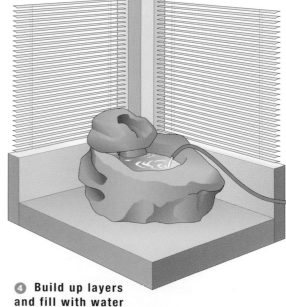

4 Build up layers and fill with water

Fatsia scandens

POINTS TO REMEMBER

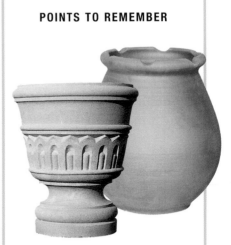

- When old ceramic sinks, terra-cotta containers, or stone urns become old and chipped, give them a new lease of life by covering them with this concrete treatment.

- It is advisable to put your feature into its final position before coating it, as it will be heavy and difficult to maneuver afterward.

- Use different sized plants to create a tiered effect behind and around the pool.

- Apply the concrete in several layers, allowing it to harden between layers.

▲ **①** *Tradescantia zebrina*, the inch plant or wandering sailor, is an excellent, fast-growing trailing plant for walls and hanging baskets in warm, reasonably bright conditions. The leaves are fleshy and often variegated.

fish wall
florarium

This spectacular wraparound panorama combines a fascinating aquarium of flickering fish with the opportunity to grow a floor-to-ceiling indoor display of exotic plants, complete with natural-looking cascade. In addition to creating a watery link between these two complementary habitats, the tumbling water adds valuable humidity and oxygen, encouraging both fish and plants to flourish.

ADVANTAGES

● Creates a personal microenvironment.

● Spectacular indoor feature combines an interest in fish and plants.

● Self-contained, it does not encroach on the room.

Keeping fish on a much smaller scale still provides a fascinating focal point and a great hobby.

There is built-in lighting overhead and the planting area is partially enclosed behind glass, with two huge circular apertures for access, so a suitably tropical microclimate can be maintained. At the same time, it usefully prevents water and plant material from soiling the room beyond. In the aquarium, a shoal of veiltails lazily explore their underwater world, with its gravel base and gently waving aquatic plants, while a lush variety of dramatic foliage plants in the florarium overhead partially conceals a large, ferny cascade. Spiky chlorophytums, dracaenas, and aloe contrast with pretty variegated peacock plants (*Calathea*), *Dieffenbachia*, and the large, heart-shaped leaves of the sweetheart plant, *Philodendron scandens*.

◄ **②** The sweetheart plant, *Philodendron scandens*, is another vigorous climber, with large, glossy heart-shaped leaves that can be up to 12 inches (30cm) long.

► **③** *Dracaena marginata* 'Tricolor' is called the rainbow plant on account of its colorful spikes of green, cream, and pink. Plants may grow to 5 feet (1.5m) in warm, reasonably light conditions.

THE CAST OF CHARACTERS

▶ ④ *Asplenium nidus*, the bird's nest fern, makes a fresh green clump of shiny fronds up to 18 inches (45cm) long and prefers warm, shady conditions.

▶ ⑥ *Peperomia caperata* is popular for its pretty heart-shaped leaves with their corrugated appearance. Different varieties produce a range of colors and flower types.

▲ ⑤ The dumb cane, *Dieffenbachia*, makes a fine display of glossy, mottled leaves. Variety *D.* 'Compacta' is ideal for smaller locations, growing to 3 feet (1m) high. The sap is poisonous so wear gloves when handling.

◀ ⑦ *Bacopa monniera*, originating from tropical and subtropical regions, grows well in an aquarium, providing it has a coarse, sandy substrate, soft- to medium-hard water, and good light.

▶ ⑧ *Chlorophytum*, the spider plant, grows well under most indoor conditions where it makes a fountain of brightly striped, straplike foliage.

◀ ⑨ *Aloe variegata*, or partridge-breasted aloe, is a pretty succulent with fleshy white-marked, pointed foliage and salmon-pink flowers from late winter to early spring. It grows only to 10 inches (26cm) high in bright, warm conditions.

▶ ⑩ *Cryptocoryne nevillii*, with its wavy green leaves, is ideal for the foreground of an aquarium, where it spreads well.

▼ ⑪ *Cryptanthus bivittatus*, the earth star plant, is a low-growing bromeliad with beautifully striped, pointed foliage. The cream stripes may turn pink in strong light. They grow well in clumps in a terrarium where plants eventually reach 6 inches (15cm) across.

▶ ⑫ *Calathea makoyana*, the peacock plant or cathedral windows, has distinctive large, pale green, oval leaves beautifully marked with darker green and tinted purple on the undersides. Plants grow to 18 inches (45cm) and require constant warmth and high humidity.

SETTING THE SCENE

FISH TANK
This two-wall aquarium is special, but there is a wide range of tanks available that can be used to create a similar effect. Many can be supplied complete with stand and integrated lighting system.

PLANTING
Containing plants behind glass, even partly, helps create a microenvironment for tropical and more tender varieties, reducing regular heating, watering, and humidity tasks. To create an exotic effect, select a good variety of foliage types, colors, and shapes, and plant them close together for a massed effect.

WATERFALL
A natural rocky cascade can look good indoors and makes a spectacular focal point among lush indoor planting. If necessary, recycle the water via a small pool at the base of the waterfall.

FISH
Keeping fish is a fascinating hobby and adds a real point of interest to a room. These veiltails—a variation of the humble goldfish—are easy to keep, but there are many exotic-looking species to choose from if you want to be more adventurous.

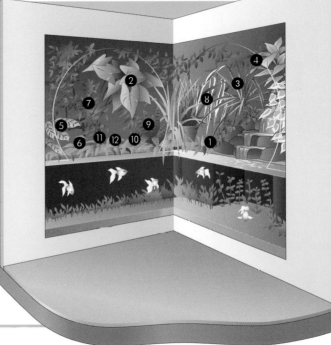

BEHIND THE SCENES

ROCKY CASCADE

A natural-looking cascade can make a fine indoor feature when combined with other garden elements such as plants and a pool. To achieve the most convincing effect, it is important to spend time positioning the rocks as naturally as possible. Alternatively, you can buy preformed cascades suitable for indoor use. For more information on aquariums, turn to pages 21–26.

Cryptanthus bivittatus

POINTS TO REMEMBER

● Use only clean rocks or boulders to keep from polluting the water.

● Make sure the structure is stable before adding plants or turning on the water.

● Allow planting pockets or shelves to position softening foliage plants.

● An indoor cascade looks best in a corner location.

1 Build up the rocks to the desired height and shape: do not make it too steep, and keep the strata of the rocks facing the same way for the most natural effect. A holding pool at the top helps maintain an even flow.

2 Line the area behind the rocks from top to bottom with a single piece of flexible pond liner. Hold it in place and hide it behind stones and boulders. Lap the bottom edge of the liner into the pool or tank at the bottom.

3 Position the waterfall outlet at the top of the cascade and conceal the feed pipe behind the stones.

4 Connect the feed pipe to the pump in the pond or tank below and turn it on: adjust the flow so that it does not spill over the sides or flow too quickly. Soften the structure with appropriate plants.

1 Build up the rocks and holding pool

2 Line the cascade

3 Position the waterfall outlet

Asplenium nidus

4 Connect to the pump and adjust the flow

BEHIND THE SCENES

WALL CASCADE

The wall cascade, the indoor version of the waterfall, makes a dramatic focal point and is quite easy to achieve, providing your pool is large enough to take the force of the water without splashing over the sides. Turn to page 18 for guidance on constructing a sunken pond.

1 Fasten the Perspex tray to the wall. Use long screws strong enough to support the tray and the weight of the water.

2 Attach the delivery hose to the pump and position it in the pool. You may need to place it on a slab or block to bring it to the correct height.

3 Position the trellis and mirror over the Perspex tray and fasten to the wall with screws.

1 Fasten the tray to the wall

2 Attach the hose to the pump

3 Position the mirror and trellis

Hebe

Chamaecyparis

POINTS TO REMEMBER

● The height and width of the cascade will determine the volume of water your pump will need to handle. If you take these calculations to your aquatics supplier, they should be able to suggest a suitable model.

● The pool must be large or deep enough for the water to be recycled quickly and the cascade kept supplied with water.

● Make sure the back wall is completely waterproof to prevent moisture from seeping behind it.

● When drilling through glass or tiles, a piece of sticky tape keeps the drill bit from slipping.

▼ **1** The white gravel underfoot that pulls the whole scheme together can be purchased by weight from landscaping and garden centers, or direct from the quarry. Other colors and sizes of stone and gravel are available for varying effects.

oriental minimalism

ADVANTAGES

● Low maintenance: plants require clipping twice a year.

● Very tranquil, relaxing atmosphere.

● Looks as good by night as by day.

Sleek metal containers are a high-tech alternative to ceramic or terra-cotta, and are the perfect foil for dramatic topiary.

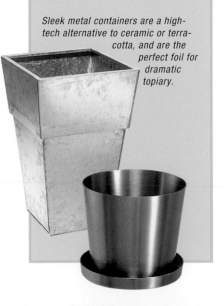

Oriental minimalism meets the gleam of high-tech in this stunning Zen-inspired corner of a modern home designed by Luciano Giubbilei. The Japanese atmosphere created by combining glass panels and black paint has been reinforced by classic elements from Zen garden philosophy: closely clipped evergreen plants, water, and rock. The overall effect is spare but creates a great sense of peace and serenity.

The pivotal feature is the water trough, cleverly constructed from glass bricks and perfectly in tune with its glass-paneled surroundings. The shiny wall-mounted sphere above is not a modern clock, but a novel, stainless steel wall fountain, mounted high on the wall to create a cascade effect. There are rocky elements in this garden interior too: a large sculptural-looking piece representing distant mountains beyond the pool, and a covering of pure white gravel across the floor. It is monochromatic, but flashes of close-cropped greenery add life and color to the scheme: box orbs in tall planters to give them height and a tall clipped evergreen tree stand sentinel beside the trough in this unusual indoor landscape.

▼ **2** Glass cannot be dismissed as simply a neutral element in the house or garden: do not underestimate its reflective qualities that give it a special affinity with water and have the effect of duplicating the greenery of plants.

▶ **3** Dense green box (*Buxus*) is ideal for topiary shapes as it has small, glossy leaves and thrives in a wide range of conditions, sun or shade. There are various forms including Japanese box, *B. microphylla* which is similar to the common European box (*B. sempervirens*) but has slightly more rounded leaves.

THE CAST OF CHARACTERS

▶ **④** The whipcord range of Hebes has small leaves and grows into neat mounds and pyramids resembling topiary forms. Most prefer a warm environment and a moist soil but will thrive in sun or shade.

◀ **⑤** Try growing and clipping small-leafed herbs such as common thyme (*Thymus vulgaris*) or silver cotton lavender (*Santolina*) into sweet-scented formal shapes.

◀ If you wish to introduce a flowering plant, go for the peace lily, *Spathiphyllum wallisiin*, that has elegant glossy leaves on long stems and superb white flowers. It is believed to filter toxins from the air. Grow it out of direct sunlight in a warm, humid room.

▶ *Selaginella* makes a closely curled carpet of bright green tufts and is a good ground cover plant for pond edges or pots and containers.

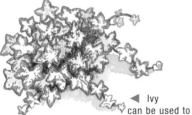

◀ Ivy can be used to clothe and soften harder features, or be trained around wire frames in imitation of topiary shapes. For growing indoors, you need to choose variations of *Hedera helix*— of which there are many including gray, green, gold, and variegated.

▼ Helxine or baby's tears is another tiny-leafed spreading plant that looks like moss.

▼ The sicklethorn, *Asparagus falcatus*, is an erect, easy-to-grow bright green plant that makes a pyramid of fine foliage.

▶ The Japanese aralia, *Fatsia japonica*, is a more showy plant with its large, hand-shaped glossy green leaves, but it creates a good effect in an oriental setting.

SETTING THE SCENE

GLASS SCREENS
The black-rimmed glass screening is essentially oriental; but might equally well be constructed from black stained timber with opaque paper panels for a less expensive, more flexible effect.

TOPIARY
Close-clipped evergreens are a typical element of the oriental garden where the domes, hummocks, and pyramids created by topiary, mosses, and conifers represent the hills and trees of the natural landscape.

GLASS POOL
Glass bricks maintain the panel effect, but have a timber rim, introducing a new, natural texture and the opportunity to conceal the return pipe for the cascade.

MODERN FOUNTAIN
The wall-mounted metal disk works on the same principle as any other wall-mounted spout, although all the fittings are kept completely hidden. Its shiny metal surface introduces a high-tech touch in a different, yet complementary reflective material.

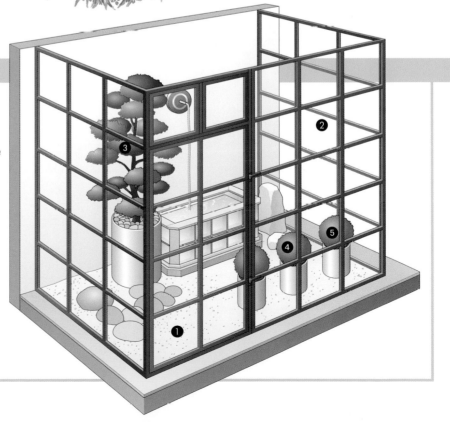

BEHIND THE SCENES

GLASS BRICK TROUGH

Glass bricks are available from builder's supply stores and are usually purchased for building bathroom shower enclosures and internal windows. You can fix them together with cement, providing you wipe any excess off the surface of the bricks immediately. For an invisible fixing and waterproof finish, use an epoxy adhesive.

❶ Make a wooden frame against the wall to construct the concrete base. Calculate the width of 2 x 2 and 2 x 5 glass bricks, depending on the size of brick you choose, and add an extra 2 inches (5 cm) around the sides and front edges. Fill the frame with concrete mix and leave to harden.

❷ Build up the sides of the trough with the glass bricks, using a clear silicone sealant to attach them to the concrete and each other. Slide a reflective aluminum sheet down the back of the trough to cover the base and back.

❸ Lower a clear acrylic or glass trough into the structure, over the aluminum sheet. Add the pump to the base of the trough, running the cable to a convenient electric point.

❹ Trim the aluminum sheet to be level with the top of the trough. Fasten metallic-painted mitered wooden beading to the corners and base with silicone sealant. As an optional extra, glue beading to cover the brick joins on the front and sides.

❺ Glue metallic-painted mitered timber to the top of the bricks with silicone sealant, leaving an overhand inside and outside of 1 to 2 inches (2.5 to 5cm) as required. Fill the trough slowly using a hose.

Ivy

❶ **Construct a concrete base**

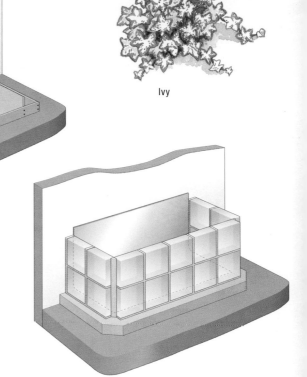

❷ **Build up glass blocks and add aluminum sheet**

❸ **Slide in watertight container and pump**

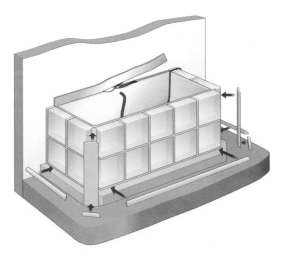

❹ **Trim aluminum sheet and add beading**

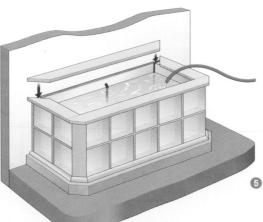

❺ **Add mitered timber and fill pool**

POINTS TO REMEMBER

● The trough will be too heavy to move once constructed, so build it in its final position.

● Clean off any smears of adhesive immediately.

● Check that the floor is strong enough to take the weight.

● Glass bricks, available from builders' merchants and bathroom suppliers, are available in a choice of colors, sizes, and finishes.

BEHIND THE SCENES

INSTALLING A POOL FOUNTAIN

A simple submersible pump is all you need to create exciting fountain effects like this one. Fountain fittings are usually supplied with a choice of spray patterns and heights, or can be channeled through an ornamental feature.

1 Connect the hose to the submersible pump and place it in position in the pool. The fountain jet unit needs to be 2–3 inches (5–8cm) above the maximum water level; if necessary, add height by putting the pump on a paving slab. To protect the liner, put the slab on a double layer of pond underlay or polyester matting.

2 Put the fountain ornament or drilled stone in position and connect the jet unit by pushing the hose up inside the fountain so that it connects with the jet. The fountain may need to be raised on a plinth; some plinths are hollow and can be used to hide the pump. Heavy fountains will only be suitable for concrete-lined or preformed pools.

3 Turn on the water and adjust the flow to ensure the fountain does not spray beyond the limits of the pool.

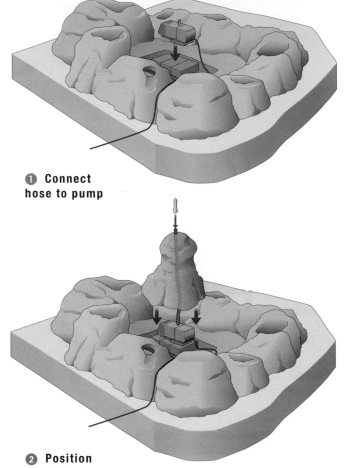

1 Connect hose to pump

2 Position fountain

3 Adjust water flow

POINTS TO REMEMBER

● Plan to keep the scale and size of your fountain to be in keeping with the pool.

● Add underwater lighting for special after-dark effects.

● If powerful enough, the same pump can be used to run other aquatic features such as a filter or cascade.

● A fountain is useful in hot weather to keep the water aerated.

FOUNTAIN OPTIONS

Plume: the classic plume fountain makes a fine architectural feature and adds height to your water feature.

Geyser: with the dramatic geyser, the water is forced into the air to greater heights and produces a louder, more foaming effect than a plume.

Column: several columns of white water create a fine moving water feature for modern pools.

Bell: bell fountains create a contained dome of water that is useful for small ponds and anywhere you don't want a lot of splash.

Bubble: bubblers are ideal for small-space water gardens, as there is no splash and the feature can be combined with pebbles, stone, or timber. With the water hidden in a concealed sump below, this feature is safe for children, too.

Special effects: with the benefit of new technology, fountains have developed into an art form, with "leaping" effects, a lattice of sprays, and even timed performances.

Tier: the traditional pyramid fountain produces continuous tiered circles of water like a watery wedding cake.

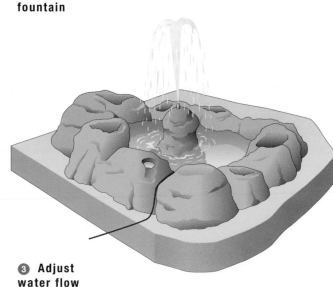

▲ **1** Flowering annuals in pots and planters add summer color and can be replaced by spring bulbs as the seasons change.

covered courtyard
pond

ADVANTAGES

● Looking good from all angles, this delightful water feature has created fine views from both buildings.

● A raised pond is easier for wheelchair users to enjoy.

● Flowering plants are grown in containers so they can be moved outside during the summer months.

● This new indoor area has made beautiful use of a wasted area.

● A large indoor pond offers the chance to grow tender water lily varieties.

A glass roof and raised formal pond have created a delightful indoor water garden where there was once only a drafty and little-used passageway between two buildings. In this new sheltered environment, center stage has been given over to a large, raised formal pond, perfectly framed by the tall walls that surround it and edged in slate to match the overall flooring.

This has produced a valuable sense of unity in what is a rather limited space. The focal point of the pond is not in the center—which is reserved for tranquil water lilies—but the eye is drawn to the simple fountain in the corner, which encourages a sense of length and perspective. The fountain adds sparkle and movement to catch the eye, while a couple of whimsical ornaments provide a personal touch. As a backdrop, a towering mass of greenery and exotic palms flourish under protection of the glass; and the changing of the seasons is marked by a careful selection of flowering shrubs and climbers such as patio roses and a Japanese quince, all helping to distract attention from the enclosing walls.

Water lilies are available in many gorgeous forms and colors, such as this Blue Beauty.

▶ **2** Slate has a soft, natural appearance, but tiles create a traditional formal look when extended over this conservatory floor and up the sides of the raised pond.

▼ A trellis is essential for supporting climbing plants and can make an attractive wall decoration in its own right, if it is well-made and stained or painted in complementary colors.

THE CAST OF CHARACTERS

▶ *Chaenomeles*, the flowering quince, is a beautiful pondside shrub for early spring reflections when red, pink, or white flowers appear on the bare branches.

▶ ④ Take advantage of an indoor pond by growing a sun-loving tropical water lily (*Nymphaea*) such as the star-shaped, rose-colored 'Independence' or popular blue and yellow 'Blue Beauty'. Equally lovely is the lotus (*Nelumbo*) which will tolerate shallower water than water lilies, but again requires plenty of sun. The American lotus, *N. lutea* is the hardiest with pale yellow blooms; for smaller ponds, look out for the dwarf lily *N. Pygmaea alba* with blooms only 4 inches (10cm) across.

◀ ③ Fan palms with their tall, strong stems and spreading heads of stiff foliage, make a spectacular display amongst massed greenery or against a brick wall. The windmill palm, *Trachycarpus fortunei*, is one of the most popular, growing well indoors providing the light is good. *Washingtonias* or American cotton palms are equally good in bright conditions, making excellent pot or tub plants. *Copernica* is a genus of 25 species of striking fan palms endemic to Cuba.

◀ ⑤ Patio roses are specially bred for their dwarf habit and massed miniature blooms. They are ideal for pots and containers and can be color-coordinated with other plants and features.

▶ Climbing plants help soften the effect of high walls and, under protection of a glassed enclosure, might include some of the more tender species such as passionflower, Californian lilac (*Ceanothus*), or fragrant Chilean jasmine, *Mandevilla laxa*.

SETTING THE SCENE

FORMAL RAISED POND
This large raised pond is central to the small conservatory area and, with its formal cladding of slate tiles, is reminiscent of Moorish inner courtyards. For a more Mediterranean feel, the slates could be replaced by patterned ceramic tiles or mosaic patterns.

FOUNTAIN
A small plume fountain is just enough to add a little life and movement in one corner of the pond without dominating other areas of interest. It leaves the center free for a carpet of flowering lilies that prefer to flourish in still water. A small fountain feature might also be a useful means of adding oxygen to the water should you wish to keep fish.

STATUE
A statue or ornamental figure seated on the side of the pond creates interesting reflections as well as a conversation piece.

MASSED GREENERY
For a lush, dramatic effect, position container foliage plants close together and add a selection of exotics such as palms and ferns; they will enjoy the proximity and thrive in their own microclimate.

BEHIND THE SCENES

RAISED FORMAL POND

When planning a formal square or rectangular pond, it pays to think big, especially if you want to add plants, ornaments, and a moving water feature such as a fountain, or maybe even fish. Once the pond is constructed, edged in hard landscaping materials, and planted up, you will be surprised how small it can look. Water's reflective qualities allow it to be used large without seeming to dominate. For more advice on raised ponds, turn to pages 16–17.

1 Prepare the footings for your pond by digging out to a depth of around 4 inches (10cm), filling with rubble, and laying a concrete pad for the base.

2 When the foundations have hardened, build up the sides of the pond in concrete blocks, checking the corners to ensure you keep your right angles true.

3 When the blockwork has set, check for rough edges. Then take a piece of black flexible liner, cut to fit the interior dimensions of the pond, and drape it over the pond. Fill slowly, using a hose and folding the liner into the corners as the weight of the water pulls it into shape.

4 When the pond is full, fold the excess liner over the top edge pond and cement slate tiles around the edge to hide it. The tiles should overhang the water slightly. Now cover the sides of the pond in the same way.

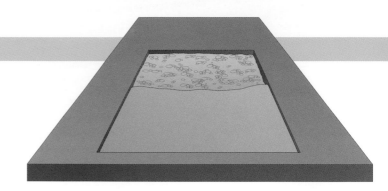

1 **Prepare base**

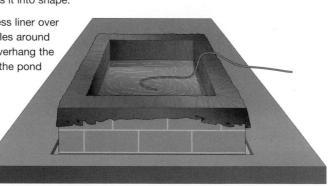

2 **Build sides**

Passion flower

3 **Drape liner and fill slowly**

4 **Hide liner with tiles**

Water lily

POINTS TO REMEMBER

• You may wish to lay the foundations and slate the floor at the same time as the pond for a seamless finish.

• To calculate how much liner you need for a square or rectangular pond, double the maximum depth of the pond and add this figure to the length. Then double the maximum depth of the pond and add it to the width. Multiply the resulting figures together for total area of liner required.

• Leave the liner overnight in a warm room before laying it, as this makes it softer and easier to manage.

• You will need to neutralize the lime content of the water using an appropriate water treatment, or drain and fill the pond twice, if any cement gets into the water.

timber and pebble
pool

▲ ❶ Hostas are popular poolside plants with their large, quilted foliage and exciting color variations—from deep blue and green, to lime green and gold. The variegated varieties with cream- or gold-edged leaves are particularly eye-catching.

ADVANTAGES

● This large area is full of interest without being overpowering.

● A formal layout where features are contained by timber decking makes maintenance minimal.

● A successful mixture of formal and informal styles meets all tastes.

This ambitious pool complex by designer Gaila Adair extends to a complete indoor water garden under glass, incorporating both traditional and more contemporary features in an unexpected blend of water, timber, stone, and glass.

To maximize its effect and usefulness, the total area has been cleverly divided into a series of overlapping sections, each used to display one of several complementary elements such as timber decking, paving, pool, and planting areas. Although the boundaries are slightly softened and blurred by a good variety of foliage, the grid effect is maintained and emphasized by bold intersecting lines of purple-stained timber.

    Central to the design is a pair of pools linked by a zigzag of decking: the one elegantly formal and strictly traditional, reserved for a tranquil spread of water lilies; the other bubbling with vitality among natural pebbles and large, colorful glass orbs. Against this dramatic framework, the planting is unexpectedly soft and natural, restricted mainly to a restful purple and yellow theme: damp-loving primulas, ferns, and hostas reinforce the water garden atmosphere, plus groups of herbs are planted for scent and color.

❷ Paving slabs create an interesting change of texture from the metal grill used in this design, and even a small paved area provides new places to walk or sit. Lay on a level bed of sand and insert creeping plants between the pavers.

▶ ❸ Sage (*Salvia officinalis*), like other herbs, has been positioned close to the decking where its spicy scent will be released when brushed against.

THE CAST OF CHARACTERS

▼ **4** Timber decking can be both a dramatic and practical feature, offering a firm, dry surface among pools and plants. It can be stained in natural shades or any color you wish for contemporary impact.

◄ **7** Primulas are a huge genus of rosette-forming plants most often seen in woodland and meadow, beside ponds and streams, where they produce a beautiful range of flowering forms. As part of a water garden planting scheme, they create a delightfully informal effect.

▲ **9** Water lilies, *Nymphaea*, will crown a still pool with beautiful lotus-like blooms, and an indoor pond provides the opportunity to grow more tender varieties. There are dwarf varieties for small pools, too.

► **8** Ferns are perfect pondside companions with their strong, feathery, deep green foliage. They grow well in containers providing you keep the soil moist. There are many indoor and outdoor types, including the elegant shuttlecock or ostrich fern, *Matteuccia struthiopteris*, whose feathery fronds make a striking, upright display of foliage.

5 Large colorful orbs floating on the water add a contemporary sculptural touch to one of the pools and are a useful focal point among more low-key features. A modern stainless steel fountain would have had a similar effect.

◄ **6** A variation on the familiar pebble fountain, here the water bubbles up among a collection of natural pebbles and modern glass orbs.

SETTING THE SCENE

FORMAL FRAMEWORK
Drawing up a framework to fit the features you want in an area can work well with a formal or semi-formal theme. Here a series of interlocking rectangles define the different areas.

TIMBER DECKING
Decking is smart and flexible, easily fitted around or over features such as water and planting areas, and provides a clean, attractive surface for walking or sitting. Here it is has been used very cleverly to surround a series of ponds and thus avoid the need for costly excavation.

POOLS
Incorporating two pools allows you to have all the water garden features you want without any clash of interests: here, the pools encompass both traditional- and contemporary-style features. Other pond owners prefer to keep a separate pool for their fish.

GLASS ORBS
The giant floating orbs in this garden are an instant focal point providing impact, shape, and color. Their effect is softened and harmonized with the rest of the garden by mixing with natural pebbles and planting.

BEHIND THE SCENES

TIMBER DECKING

Its esthetic qualities and designer possibilities aside, decking must be safely constructed and maintained, and it must be non-slip. You can buy the components from DIY and specialist shops, or construct your own. There is a grooved, non-slip version which is worth placing beside a pond.

Timber decking must be solidly constructed and regularly maintained for safety. If you need to raise it above 1 foot (30cm), it is advisable to consult a professional joiner. Laying on the diagonal in different directions, or staining and bleaching, can create stylish effects to coordinate with other garden features.

1 The supporting piers should be firmly built on concrete foundations. Dig out to around 15 inches (38cm) square and fill with 4:1 concrete mix. Allow to set.

2 Build up the piers to the necessary height using concrete blocks or bricks.

3 Fasten the supporting joists or subframe to the piers with galvanized straps.

4 Fix the decking planks to the subframe using galvanized screws, leaving a gap of around ½ inch (1.3cm) between the planks for rain run-off.

POINTS TO REMEMBER

- You can use softwood or hardwood to construct your decking; softwood is less expensive, but will need more frequent maintenance.

- Slightly overlapping timber over the edge of a pond will make it look as though the water flows beneath.

- An area of decking can be joined to the house or any other building using coach bolts, providing there is a drainage channel between the junctions.

- Supporting piers should be positioned about 3 feet (1m) apart.

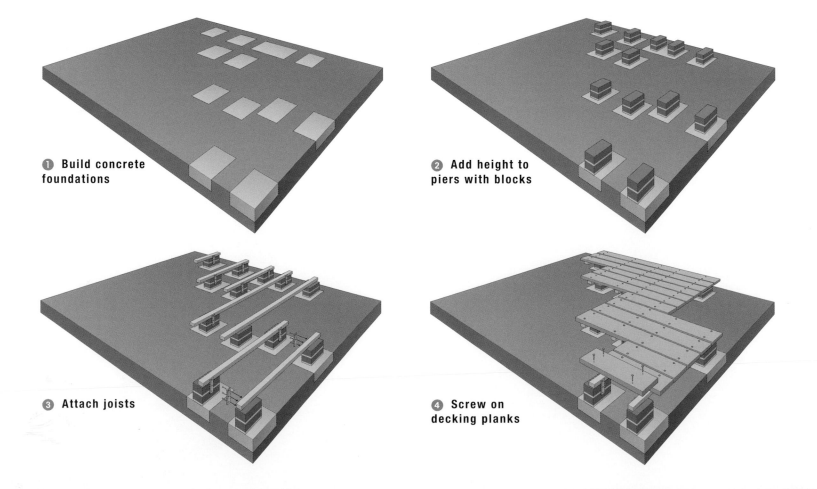

1 Build concrete foundations

2 Add height to piers with blocks

3 Attach joists

4 Screw on decking planks

BEHIND THE SCENES

TILING

Tiles are hard-wearing, waterproof, and available in a wide range of textures and finishes from natural stone, slate, granite or marble, to plain and patterned ceramics. They are an excellent way to line or edge an indoor pool, especially when they can be coordinated with surrounding decorative features. For further advice on sunken pools, turn to page 18.

1 To attach tiles to a vertical surface, begin by marking the upper edge of the area to be tiled using a pencil and level, and the vertical edge with a plumb line. For floor tiles, work out where the first line of complete tiles will run from (usually on the far side of your main viewing point) and draw your line there. Generally, tiling looks better if you start in the center of the row and work outward.

2 Apply tile adhesive with a comb spreader to a manageable area.

3 Start pressing the tiles firmly into position by sliding them downward, using wooden nibs or plastic spacers between the tiles to make sure they are evenly spaced. Some modern tiles are self-spacing and can be butted up together without the need for spacers.

4 When the tile adhesive is dry, apply a suitable grout to the spaces between, using a rubber spreader. As you finish each section, wipe excess grout from the tiles immediately with a sponge.

5 To make a clean break in a tile, score with a glass cutter, then place the tile over two matchsticks or nails. Tap sharply and the tile should snap neatly in two.

6 To cut ceramic tiles into more irregular shapes, use special tile pincers to nibble away a small amount at a time until you achieve the required shape.

POINTS TO REMEMBER

● Apply tiles only to a sound, properly prepared surface. Score smooth surfaces with a piece of hardened steel if necessary for a better "key" for the adhesive.

● Never assume that other features in the room such as skirting boards and door frames are straight. Double-check using your level and plumb line.

● Use only nonslip tiles for floor areas.

● Clean away excess grout or adhesive immediately from the surface of your tiles.

● Calculate the number of tiles required carefully. You should allow around 10 percent extra for breakages and errors.

2 Apply tile adhesive

3 Press tiles into position

4 Apply grout and clean tiles

1 Mark up the area

5 Breaking a tile in half

6 Shaping a tile

BEHIND THE SCENES

A SMALL ARCHED BRIDGE

An arched bridge is more difficult to make than a level one, but it makes a very pretty feature spanning a suitable stretch of water. You are unlikely to find an off-the-shelf model small enough for indoor use, so you will have to order one custom-made or make your own. This variation on the bridge in the main photograph is made of steel, with wooden treads.

1 Order two pieces of 2-inch (5-cm) outside diameter 10-gauge steel pipe to the length required plus 3 feet (1m). Ask for them to be rolled into a curve to span the area required. Weld a 12-inch (30-cm) mild steel plate onto each end of the pipes.

2 Excavate enough at either end of the bridge for the poles to be inserted 18 inches (46cm) into a concrete pad. Pour in a 4:1 concrete mix and bed the poles in position. When the concrete is set, backfill and level the floor.

3 Depending on the size of your bridge, weld three or four sections of 2 x ⅛ inch (50 x 8mm) flat steel at intervals between the two poles.

4 Weld two more sections of flat steel running the length of the bridge to these cross bearers.

5 Your tread timbers can now be screwed onto these supporting joists.

6 Trim the timbers to the shape of the bridge, and stain or paint to finish.

1 **Sections of steel pipe are rolled into a curve**

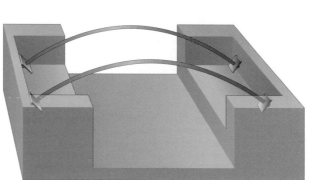

2 **Insert pipe into a concrete pad**

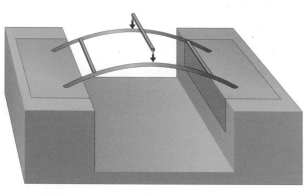

3 **Weld cross sections to the main structure**

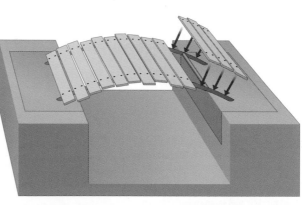

4 **Screw tread timbers to the frame**

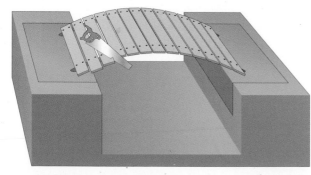

5 **Trim the timbers to shape**

Nelumbo

POINTS TO REMEMBER

● When calculating the finished length of your bridge, don't forget to allow room to excavate without damaging the pond.

● If the bridge is to be used rather than just ornamental, it needs to be strongly and safely constructed as detailed here, with the foundations concreted into the ground. An ornamental bridge might simply require brackets for fixing.

● Angling the ends of the pipe slightly when fixing into the ground will alter the shape of the curve and produce a more 'humpbacked' effect.

● Use only galvanized screws for fixing the timbers. Check screws and timbers regularly for wear.

the directories

Choosing the right plants and fish for your indoor water feature can be bewildering. Certain plants prefer warmer rooms and direct sunlight, while some species of fish cannot bear to be in the same tank. Make sure that your choice fits your feature and its environment, and learn how to maintain feature, fish, and plants to provide years of trouble-free enjoyment.

◀ Dramatic planting, such as this Kaffir lily (*Clivia miniata*), can be a major attraction of an indoor water feature.

how to use the *plant* directory

An indoor pool or fountain provides the perfect opportunity to grow tender aquatic species as well as an interesting range of complementary house and conservatory plants. If you plan your display carefully, with a good mixture of foliage and flower shapes, sizes, and colors, you can achieve a superb effect that will give you year-round pleasure.

Except for the small tabletop fountains and freestanding ornaments, it will be your choice and position of plants, plus good maintenance, that will ensure the success of your indoor water garden. Apart from the indisputable attraction of foliage and flowers, they help to soften your feature's construction and can even be used to establish a certain atmosphere: maybe a Mediterranean kitchen/diner with lots of herbs and terra-cotta pots around a mini-fountain, an oriental-style living room complete with still pool and elegant bamboos in baskets, or a mass of palms and feathery ferns around a rocky cascade in a junglelike setting.

Your initial choice must take into account each plant's needs for light, heat, and humidity, and ensure your selection prefers a similar habitat: it will be no good grouping humidity-loving tropicals with a collection of cacti that prefer hot, dry conditions, for example, as you will never be able to satisfy both groups. Once you have decided upon the effect you want to create, you should be looking at a good basic framework of foliage species. Try to achieve a variety of shapes by blending tall spiky plants with large foliage ones at the rear of your design and having feathery or tiny-leaved plants softening the planting at the front. If you can't afford too many large specimens, use plant stands, shelving, or staging to produce a multi-tiered effect. Flowering plants tend to be shorter-lived and are useful for adding seasonal splashes of color to your arrangement if required: you can use container-grown spring bulbs in the same way.

① — *Nymphaea* — **②**
(Water Lily)
③ — **Size: varies with variety**

An indoor pool is the perfect opportunity to grow one or more tropical water lilies, which, if grown in the right conditions, can flower from early summer to winter. The size varies from the giant tropical *N. gigantea* with pads more than 2 feet (60cm) across, to *N. pygmaea*, whose leaves measure 12 inches (30cm) across. There are many types and colors to choose from; all are bewitchingly scented and some even bloom only at night. Grow in special planting baskets of a mixture of half loam-based compost and well-rotted manure with a little added high-phosphate fertilizer on the bottom of the pool. Cover the compost with gravel, leaving just the top of the crown uncovered. **④**

The directory shows:

① The plant's botanical name in Latin—this is international and is the name usually used in nurseries and garden centers.

② The plant's common name—this is the name used by most people to refer to the plant.

③ The plant's approximate height when fully grown, in imperial and metric measurements.

④ General information—this gives details of the plant's characteristics and cultivation requirements.

GUIDE TO SYMBOLS

Plants in this directory have been coded with one of the following symbols to provide instant recognition of its general type and use, to help with your selection.

 Good foliage plants
Plants with dramatic or interesting foliage (e.g., ferns or palms) for creating an exciting contrast of shapes.

Flowering plants
Flowering plants (e.g., violets or geraniums) that are useful for adding seasonal scent and/or color.

 Trailing/climbing plants
Climbing and trailing plants (e.g., ivy or jasmine) that can be encouraged to soften walls and containers.

Aquatic plants
Aquatic species (e.g., water lilies) that prefer to grow in or near the water.

BUYING AND PLANTING TIPS

● Bring plants home immediately after you have bought them; do not leave to wilt in a hot car.

● Buy from a good garden center or florist shop where the plants are well cared for and healthy looking. Never buy from displays outside supermarkets and gas stations, as these plants may be subject to neglect, drafts, and pollution from passing traffic.

● Check each plant's needs and position accordingly.

● Keep soil out of ponds and pools when maintaining plants to avoid polluting the water.

PLANTS FOR INDOOR POOLS

Most require good light and a room temperature between 55°F (13°C) and 90°F (32°C).

Acorus gramineus 'Variegatus'
(Japanese Rush)
Height: 2½ ft (75cm)

An attractive marginal for unheated ponds, this plant has tufts of green and white striped leaves. Grow in pots of loam-based compost submerged below the water's surface on a purpose-built marginal shelf or supported on bricks or blocks.

Cyperus alternifolius
(Galingale, Umbrella Sedge)
Height: 3 ft (1m)

A tall elegant plant with umbrellalike clusters of flowers and slender leaves, it is suitable for the pond shallows and requires temperatures of 54°F (12°C) or more. There is an attractive variegated version, *'Variegatus'*, and a compact form, *C. haspan*. Root in pots of loam-based compost.

Aponogeton
(Latticeleaf)

Sometimes called latticeleaf because of its pronounced network of veining on the long, submerged 6 inch (15cm) leaves, this is an underwater plant that requires good light and temperatures of at least 60°F (16°C). It must be grown in a loam-based compost.

Eichhornia crassipes
(Water Hyacinth)

Grown for its beautiful mauve clusters of hyacinthlike flowers, this plant thrives in the muddy water at the bottom of a pool or tank and does not need to be rooted. It is a pernicious weed in the wild, so take advantage of the chance to grow it indoors in more controlled conditions.

Elodea
(Pondweed, Waterweed)
Length: 10 ft (3m)
Spread: indefinite

This fine oxygenating plant will grow well in most temperatures in loam-based compost in pools or tanks. Choose between E. crispa (now called Lagarosiphon major) with shorter stems, and the larger E. densa (now called Egeria densa), or Brazilian waterweed.

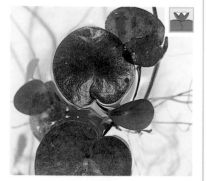

Hydrocharis
morsus-ranae
(Frogbit)
Spread: 3ft (1m)

This is a pretty floating plant for small pools with its tiny, round lilylike foliage and small white flowers. It is tolerant of a wide range of temperatures.

Myriophyllum
proserpinacoides
(Parrot's Feather)
Length: 6 ft (1.8m) stems

The fresh blue-green foliage of this aquatic plant responds well to the warmer conditions indoors and is a good oxygenator. The leaves turn red in fall.

Nymphaea
(Water Lily)
Size: varies with variety

An indoor pool is the perfect opportunity to grow one or more tropical water lilies, which, if grown in the right conditions, can flower from early summer to winter. The size varies from the giant tropical N. gigantea with pads more than 2 feet (60cm) across, to N. pygmaea, whose leaves measure 12 inches (30cm) across. There are many types and colors to choose from; all are bewitchingly scented and some even bloom only at night. Grow in special planting baskets of a mixture of half loam-based compost and well-rotted manure with a little added high-phosphate fertilizer on the bottom of the pool. Cover the compost with gravel, leaving just the top of the crown uncovered.

Orontium aquaticum
(Golden Club)
Spread: 2 ft (60cm)

This unusual-looking aquatic with its arumlike bright yellow flowers held 4 inches (10cm) above the water should be grown in aquatic baskets of half loam-based compost and half well-rotted manure positioned about 1 foot (30cm) deep. It is reasonably temperature tolerant.

Pistia stratiotes
(Water Lettuce)
Height and Spread: 4 in (10cm)

This floating plant with its pale green rosettes of foliage and tiny flowers requires a temperature of around 70°F (21°C) and some shade in summer.

Pontederia cordata
(Pickerel Weed)
Height: 2½ ft (75cm)
Spread: 1½ ft (45cm)

This most attractive marginal plant with its glossy green heart-shaped leaves and mass of bright blue flowers is tolerant of most temperatures and can be grown in baskets of half loam-based compost and half rotted manure in less than 1 foot (30cm) of water.

Zantedeschia aethiopica
(Arum Lily)
Height: 3 ft (1m)

This tropical-looking lily will transform the simplest pool with its spectacular white lily flowers and glossy arrow-shaped leaves rising up at the water's edge. Plant it in 1- or 2-gallon containers filled with rich soil and set it in water that is up to 2 inches (5cm) over the crown. They will need sun or partial shade.

PLANTS FOR MODERATELY HEATED ROOMS

Plants for moderately heated conservatories and living rooms maintaining a temperature above 50°F (10°C) at night and up to 60°F (15°C) during the day.

Aporocactus flagelliformis
(Rat's Tail Cactus)
Height: 3 ft (1m)

This is an excellent plant for hanging baskets: long spiny stems produce bright pink flowers. This plant is easy to grow but prefers a peat-based compost and a moist soil. Feed regularly in summer.

Bougainvillea
(Bougainvillea)
Height: 8 ft (2.5m)

If you grow this tender climber with its distinctive red, yellow, pink or orange bracts in a large pot of loam-based compost in full light, it may reach 5–8 feet (1.5–2.5m) across a conservatory roof. It needs regular watering and ventilation in summer; allow to rest in winter.

Citrus
Height: 4 ft (1.2m)

As long as you keep the soil moist and provide shade in summer, both *C. limon*, a dwarf lemon, and *C. mitis*, or *Calamondin* orange, will make attractive evergreen shrubs for pots and tubs. The plant needs high humidity, so mist regularly (but mind not to overwater).

Clivia miniata
(Kaffir Lily)
Height: 2 ft (60cm)

Dark green straplike leaves and large clusters of trumpet-shaped red and yellow flowers make this a fine pot plant. Water sparingly in winter, allowing the soil to remain almost dry. Water well in summer.

Asplenium
(Spleenwort; Hen and chicken fern [*bulbiferum*]; Bird's nest fern [*australasicum*])
Height: Between 2-3 ft (0.5-1m); Spread: Between 8-12 in (20-30cm)

A pretty fern with fresh green colored fronds. It grows best in peat-based compost and prefers humid conditions. Shade from direct sunlight.

Chlorophytum comosum 'Vittatum'
(Spider Plant)
Height and Spread: 1 ft (30cm) Stems and plantlets may reach 6 ft (1.8m) long

Easy to grow and tolerant of a wide range of conditions, the arching white-striped leaves and drooping stems of little plantlets look good in hanging baskets or pedestal pots.

Clianthus puniceus
(Parrot's Bill)
Height: 6–12 ft (1.8–3.6m)

The unusual bright red flowers are set off by the feathery evergreen foliage. It is best planted in pots of loam-based compost.

Codiaeum variegatum var. pictum
(Croton, South Sea Laurel)
Height: 3 ft (1m)

Grown for its brightly patterned foliage, this plant needs heat and humidity. Shade from direct sunlight, but move to a sunny spot in winter. Mist-spray regularly in warm weather.

Cymbidium
(Orchid)
Height: 2–2½ ft (60–75cm)

This clump-forming orchid has showy flowers of varying shades of pink, yellow or white and can be increased by division. Grow in pots of specially formulated orchid compost and keep moist, but allow to dry out in winter.

Echinocactus grusonii
(Golden Barrel)
Diameter: 3–9 in (8–20cm)

This large, round cactus has strong yellowish spines along the ribs. Grow in a sunny, well-ventilated position in formulated cactus mixture, and allow to dry out between waterings.

Hibiscus rosa-sinensis
(Rose Mallow, Chinese Hibiscus, Shoeflower)
Height: 6ft (1.8m)
Can grow to 15ft (4.5m)

There are many hybrids available of this superb evergreen shrub with its glossy dark green leaves and showy flowers of pink, red, or yellow. Grow in pots of loam-based compost and protect from direct sunlight. Water frequently in summer.

Kalanchoe tubiflora
(Chandelier Plant)
Height: 3ft (1m)

The succulent brown-spotted, gray-green leaves are cylindrical, producing clusters of hanging pink-orange-red flowers. Keep moist except during the winter months.

Dieffenbachia Amoena
(Giant Dumb Cane)
Height: 6 ft (1.8m)

This fine foliage plant has large, dark green, glossy leaves with white veining up to 1½ ft (45cm) long. It likes warm, humid conditions and a peat-based compost. Feed regularly in summer. This plant is poisonous.

Echinocereus cinerascens
(Hedgehog Cactus)
Height: 1 ft (30cm)

This branched cactus produces bright pinkish purple flowers in a warm, sunny position with good ventilation. Allow the compost to dry out between waterings.

Ipomoea acuminata
(Morning Glory)
Height: 20 ft (6m)

Grown in pots or raised beds, this perennial climber will produce purple-blue flowers that turn pink over a long period. The seeds are poisonous.

Lithops bella
(Living Stones)
Height: ¾–1¼ in (2–3cm);
Spread: ⅝ in (1.5cm)

This curious plant really does look like a pile of pebbles from which white daisylike flowers surprisingly bloom. It needs to be kept dry during the winter months.

Monstera deliciosa
(Swiss Cheese Plant)
Height: 20–25 ft (6–7.5m)

In a warm conservatory, this large, popular houseplant with huge, holey leaves will reach its maximum height. It prefers a moist, peat-based compost, and needs the support of a moss stick, which should be kept moist by spraying.

Pelargonium
(Geranium)
**Height: 6 in–3 ft (15cm–90cm)
according to type**

A large genus of popular plants, some geraniums are grown for their showy flowers and others for their silver-marked green foliage. Grow in peat-based compost in semi-shaded, humid conditions.

Plumbago auriculata
(Leadwort)
Height: 10–20 ft (3–6m)

This evergreen climbing plant is covered with pretty blue flowers in summer. Grow in pots or raised beds of loam-based compost and tie to a suitable support. Prefers bright light in cool conditions.

Rhoicissus rhomboidea
(African Grape Ivy)
Height: 20ft (6m)

This popular climber with dark green foliage is easily pruned. Grow in pots of loam-based compost in semi-shade. It requires ventilation in summer and some support for the tendrils to twine around.

Passiflora caerulea
(Blue Passion Flower, Blue Crown Passion Flower)
Height: 30 ft (9m)

This lovely flowering climber requires good support and produces blue flowers and yellow non-edible fruits. In other varieties the fruits are purple and delicious.

Platycerium bifurcatum
(Staghorn Fern)
Height and Spread: 3 ft (1m)

This is a fine exotic-looking fern which will grow in hanging baskets or attached to a piece of bark. Water well in spring and summer, but keep drier through the winter months.

Pteris cretica
(Cretan Brake, Ribbon Fern)
**Height: 18 in (45cm)
Spread: 12 in (30cm)**

This clump-forming evergreen fern has delicate feathery fronds, sometimes with white centers. Grow in pots of peat-based compost.

Saintpaulia ionantha
(African Violet)
**Height: 4 in (10cm)
Spread: 10 in (25cm)**

Pretty purple, blue, or pink-violet flowers grow in the center of a rosette of thick, feltlike leaves. Grow in a warm, draft-free position and allow the compost to dry out between waterings.

PLANTS FOR HEATED ROOMS

Plants for heated conservatories and plant rooms with a minimum temperature at night of 60°F (16°C), a daytime temperature of 60–70°F (16–21°C), and high humidity.

Sedum
(Stonecrop)
**Height: 3 in–1 ft (7.5–30cm)
according to type
Spread: indefinite**

These succulent plants with their massed decorative foliage are easy to grow in well-drained compost. Allow the soil to dry out between each watering and water sparingly in winter. *S. morganianum* (Burro's Tail, Donkey's Tail) is popular for its curtain of blue-green leafy stems when grown in a hanging basket.

Senecio x hybridus
(Cineraria)
**Height: 12 in (30cm)
Spread: 12 in (30cm)**

This flowering pot plant is popular for its daisylike, brightly colored flowers and large, roundish leaves. It prefers a loam-based compost, good ventilation, and shade from direct sunlight.

Strelitzia reginae
(Bird of Paradise)
Height: 3–4 ft (1–1.2m)

The tall clump of evergreen leaves on long stalks produces striking orange and blue flowers horizontal to the end of the stem. Plant in bright light for the most flowers, or in shade for the best-looking foliage.

Thunbergia alata
(Black-Eyed Susan)
Height: 10 ft (3m)

A pretty twining climber with distinctive white, cream, or orange flowers with dark centers. It prefers a warm slightly humid atmosphere and shade from direct sunshine.

Adiantum
(Maidenhair Fern)
**Height and Spread: 1–4 ft
(30cm–1.2m) according to type**

This elegant fern needs shade but likes the warmth of a heated conservatory. There are many varieties which will grow well in moist, but not saturated, peat-based compost.

Anthurium andraeanum
(Flamingo Lily, Oilcloth Flower)
**Height: 24–30 in (60–75cm)
Spread: 20 in (50cm)**

This exotic tropical flowering plant needs a mixture of half peat-based compost and half sphagnum moss, and warm, humid conditions away from direct sunlight. Flowers vary from orange or scarlet with a yellow spadix, to pink and white, according to variety.

Browallia speciosa
(Sapphire Flower)
Height: 4 ft (1.2m)

This attractive flowering plant can be grown as an annual. The flowers are deep blue, although there is a white variety called 'Silver Bells'.

Cordyline terminalis
(Tree of Heaven)
Height: 10ft (3m)

Give this exotic bronze-green tree warmth, humidity and a loam-based compost, and it may grow to its maximum height. Varieties offer a choice of leaf color including pink, cream, and green.

Clerodendrum thomsoniae
(Bleeding Heart Vine)
Height: 10–12 ft (3–3.4m)

A handsome flowering climber for warm, humid conditions, the flowers are red and white. It needs to be shaded from direct sunlight and grown in a large container or indoor bed of loam- or peat-based compost.

Mimosa pudica
(Sensitive Plant, Touchmendt)
Height: 3 ft (1m)

This small, shrubby perennial makes a pretty foliage plant whose graceful leaves fold up when touched, hence its common name. It needs partial shade and warm conditions. Water liberally during the growing period, but sparingly in the winter.

Neoregelia carolinae/ N. marechalii
(Blushing Bromeliad, Heart of Flame)
Height: 8–12 in (20–30cm)
Spread: 16–24 in (40–60cm)

This evergreen bromeliad makes a bright green, dense rosette with a red center. The leaves can be 16 inches (40cm) long. Grow in small pots of peat-based compost, keeping the center of the rosettes filled with water. The variety 'Tricolor' has striped cream and pink leaves.

Phalaenopsis amabilis
(Moth Orchid)
Height: 2 ft (60cm)

The flowers of this thick-stemmed orchid have white petals with yellow centers marked in red. The sparse leaves can be 10 inches (25cm) long.

Ficus benjamina
(Weeping Fig)
Height: 6 ft (1.8m)

Grown in a peat-based compost and given warmth, humidity, and shade, this weeping evergreen makes a graceful tree of elegant green foliage. Other figs which make handsome container-grown house or conservatory plants include *F. elastica* (Rubber Plant) and *F. pumila* (Climbing Fig), which will grow in cooler conditions.

Musa acuminata
(Chinese Banana)
Height: 7–8 ft (2.1–2.4m)

This shorter variety of the huge commercial banana makes a fine container plant with its giant green, shiny fronds. Grow in loam-based compost in a warm, humid atmosphere out of direct sunlight.

Paphiopedilum callosum
(Lady's Slipper)
Height: 3 in (7.5cm)

This is a large-flowered orchid with distinctive pouch-shaped blooms in shades of white, green, purple, red, and pink. The straplike leaves have a black spotted effect. Keep humid and shade from direct sunlight.

Sansevieria trifasciata
(Mother-in-Law's Tongue, Snake Plant)
Height: 2–4 ft (60–120cm)

Grown for its stiff foliage with its green and silver markings, warm conditions will encourage this popular houseplant to reach its maximum height.

Schefflera actinophylla
(Australian Umbrella Tree)
Height: 8 ft (2.4m) in tubs

The leaflets radiate from a central stem to make an attractive foliage plant. Keep warm and humid, feeding regularly during the growing season.

Schlumbergera x buckleyi
(Christmas Cactus)
Height: Stems 1 ft (30cm) long

Popular for its trumpet-shaped, deep pink winter flowers which sprout from the joints along the flat, fleshy stems, this epiphytic cactus can be grown at lower temperatures but does best in a warm environment. Allow the soil to dry out between each watering. It needs good light conditions in winter, but keep out of direct sun in summer.

Scindapsus aureus
(Epipremnum aureum)
(Devil's Ivy)
Height: 6–10 ft (1.8–3m)

This attractive climber is grown for its bright green, shiny leaves patterned with yellow. It needs warmth and humidity, and shade in summer. Grow in peat-based compost and provide a moss stick for support.

Stephanotis floribunda
(Madagascar Jasmine)
Height: 16 ft (5m)

This vigorous climber with oval evergreen leaves is grown for its lovely scented white flowers. It does best in a warm location in pots of loam-based compost. Feed regularly in summer and do not overwater in winter.

PLANTS FOR UNHEATED ROOMS

Plants for unheated rooms or conservatories where the temperature may fall below freezing, but where some form of heating will be employed during long, cold periods.

Camellia japonica
(Camellia)
Height: 20 ft (6m)

This lovely flowering evergreen makes a good pot plant, providing the container is large and includes only lime-free compost. The superb flowers are 3–5 inches (7.5–12cm) across and may be single or double, in shades of red, orange, pink, or white. After flowering, dig in the pots outdoors and bring indoors again in fall. Prune in late spring to keep in check.

Campanula isophylla
(Italian Bellflower)
Height: 4 in (10cm)
Spread: 12 in (30cm)

A fine trailing plant for shelves and hanging baskets, the slender stems are covered in blue or white star-shaped flowers in late summer. Grow in loam-based compost in a well-ventilated and well-lighted position.

Campsis grandiflora
(Chinese Trumpet Creeper)
Height: 30 ft (9m)

This exotic climber grows well in an indoor bed or border, where it will produce a mass of scarlet flowers in late summer. Grow in well-drained but moist soil.

Cyclamen persicum
(Cyclamen)
Height: 4–8 in (10–20cm)
Spread: 6–8 in (15–20cm)

This delightful flowering pot plant offers a wide range of colors from reds and pinks to white. Some varieties have bicolored foliage, too. Grow in a peat-based compost away from direct sunlight, do not overwater, and maintain at a temperature between 45 and 60°F (7 and 16°C).

Fatsia japonica
(Japanese Fatsia)
Height: 5 ft (1.5m)

This dramatic foliage plant makes a bold statement with its glossy green hand-shaped leaves that grow to around 9–12 inches (22–30cm) across.

Hedera spp.
(Ivy)

Ivies make excellent creeping, climbing, and trailing plants for cooler locations. They are easy to grow and available in a wide range of foliage shapes, sizes, colors, and patterns, including variegated forms. Shade from direct sunlight.

Jasminum polyanthum
(Jasmine)
Height: 10 ft (3m)

This useful semi-evergreen twining plant produces many fragrant flowers between winter and spring. Grow in an indoor planting bed or in a large container and keep moist.

Lilium spp.
(Lily)
**Height: 3–6 ft (1–1.8m)
according to species**

Elegant lilies look superb in a formal setting or beside a formal pool. Grow in pots of loam-based compost, water freely, and feed regularly once the bulbs begin to grow. Keep well ventilated and shade from strong sunlight. There are many beautiful forms to choose from; some blooms may be scented, too.

Fuchsia spp.
(Fuchsia)
Height: 2–5 ft (60 cm–1.5m)

This popular flowering pot plant offers hundreds of variations in flower type and color. The plant may be tall, pendulous, or dwarfed. Grow in loam-based compost in tubs or hanging baskets and feed regularly during the summer months. Plants can also be bought or trained as standards.

Hydrangea macrophylla
(Hydrangea)
**Height: 5–6 ft (1.5–1.8m);
Spread: 6–8 ft (I.8–2.5m)**

This showy flowering pot plant has a large number of varieties. The individual flowerheads are huge and come in shades of blue, red, white, and pink. Keep moist and shade from strong sunlight.

Lapageria rosea
(Chilean Bellflower)
Height: 16 ft (5m)

This exotic flowering twiner produces waxy bell-shaped pink flowers from summer to fall. It prefers a moist but not saturated, peat-based compost.

Sarracenia flava
(Pitcher Plant)
Height: 1½ ft (45cm)

This unusual carnivorous plant is grown for its yellow-green rosettes of flowers and strange-looking tubular flowers. Grow in pans of half peat-based compost and half sphagnum moss, and keep moist and humid, away from direct sunlight.

fish directory

If you are planning an indoor water feature such as a pond or pool, why not extend your interest further and start a new hobby: fishkeeping. Fish add color and life to the water and will soon become tame enough to come to the side of the pool at feeding time, offering hours of pleasure and companionship.

▲ Large, handsome, and tame enough to feed by hand, keeping koi is an exciting hobby.

Pump with filter and UV

Providing you take care not to overstock, and maintain good water quality with the help of filters and aerators, there is no reason you should not keep hardy fish like goldfish and koi in larger indoor pools. Some koi keepers even maintain both indoor and outdoor ponds, which may be linked under a conservatory wall, so that the fish can move freely between home and garden. Or if you fancy observing something a bit more exotic and at closer quarters, there is a wide range of attractive and unusual species you can keep in an aquarium (see page 25 for setting up an aquarium).

PREPARING THE POND OR AQUARIUM

The first rule is to make sure the pond (or aquarium) is ready for occupancy before you buy any livestock. In nature a complex ecological process keeps the water clean and at the correct biological level, but you will have to achieve this with the help of filters, refills, and chemical correctors. Fish need an alkaline pH between 7.3 and 8.0; you should test your pond before you introduce any fish, and weekly thereafter, using a proprietary pH test kit. Kits are also available for assessing the ammonia or nitrite levels of your pond; these are pollutants that tend to build up as a result of fish waste. Replacing around 10 percent of the water every two weeks and using a filter to process the toxins should help keep your fish happy and healthy.

To operate, pond filters require an electric pump capable of circulating the total volume of the pond every two hours; they remove any solid matter suspended in the water and, in time, grow a colony of beneficial bacteria that helps to maintain good water quality by breaking down the toxins excreted by the fish. An ultraviolet unit fitted to the filter (some models already incorporate a UV) will help to prevent the water in ponds and aquariums that receive plenty of light from turning green. Good filtration is essential, and it is a good idea to have a spare pump in case the one in use stops working. In hot weather, fish need well-oxygenated water, too.

If your pond is in a sunny position, near a window, or in a conservatory, it may have to be shaded using blinds or good plant cover. This is not only to stop it from overheating, but will

▲ Test kits help keep pH and ammonia levels in check.

also prevent oxygen supplies from becoming depleted and—most importantly—inhibits the growth of single-celled algae and blanketweed (the latter UV will not touch). Anything below 8 parts oxygen per million (ppm) and your fish will start coming to the surface gulping air. Ideally they like 15ppm. A small fountain will help keep oxygen levels up, but even more reliable is a small bubbler or aerator which can be left on as required. Best of all is a small waterfall which has a large air/water interfacer.

Introduce your fish singly or in pairs, building up stocks gradually, and make sure that the fish you buy are top-quality stock that look lively and healthy and have no sign of disease or listlessness. If you can, quarantine new fish for several weeks in a holding tank that is equally well aerated and filtered to keep from introducing infection. Make sure you don't overstock your pond or aquarium.

Fountain

FISH STOCKING LEVELS

Generally speaking, you should allow 1 inch (2.5cm) of fish per 2 square inches (12.5 sq.cm) of water surface; or 10 in (25cm) of fish per 100 gallons (455l).

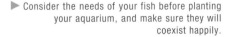
▲ Your fish will appreciate some weed cover to hide and breed in.

▶ Consider the needs of your fish before planting your aquarium, and make sure they will coexist happily.

▲ You can enjoy a fine display of fish, flowers, and clear, healthy water if you keep the pond well filtered and aerated.

FISH HEALTH

Regular maintenance and good water quality are key to healthy fish stocks. Back this up with correct feeding and keep a sharp eye on the general condition of your fish. A wide range of food is available, some recommended for certain types of fish, including flakes, freeze-dried, pellets, pastes, sticks, and frozen live foods such as bloodworms, daphnia, krill, and shrimp. Usually you get what you pay for and the better-quality preparations tend to be the most nutritious. You can cut costs by joining a local fishkeepers' club and buying in bulk. Store the food in a cool, dry place in a sealed container and check the "use by" dates.

Quantity and frequency are the key to efficient feeding; you do not want your fish to gorge themselves, nor to be left with undigested food in the water, which will act as a pollutant. Follow the manufacturer's instructions. Generally about 2 percent of their body weight per day is a good rule of thumb. As a guide for pond fish: a 4-inch (10-cm) koi or goldfish weighs around 6 ounces (170 grams), and a 12-inch (30-cm) fish weighs about 26 ounces (737 grams). Little and often tends to be the best approach. You can buy electronically controlled timed feeders if this does not suit your personal schedule.

Fish have a natural immune system that will fend off most pathogens (disease-causing organisms). Should this immunity be reduced on account of poor water quality, stress, or physical damage, they may quickly fall prey to bacterial, viral, fungal, or parasitic attack. Check regularly for symptoms such as reddened or ragged fins, ulcers, and raised scales. Some minor bacterial ailments like these can be treated by improving pond hygiene, carrying out regular partial water changes, and applying a proprietary bactericide. If the problem persists, contact a veterinarian or the infection will pass quickly from one fish to another. Scratches and scrapes from rubbing on rocks or clumsy handling can result in fungal infections that take the form of a woolly-looking coating which spreads over the fins and body. Treat as soon as detected. White spot is another killer of pond fish, but this can be eradicated if spotted and treated soon enough. Also keep an eye out for signs of listlessness or irritably flicking motions which indicate the presence of parasites such as flukes. Treat these with the appropriate remedy.

Feeding ring

Floating foodsticks

Flake food mix

▲ Healthy fish are lively, unblemished, and a good color.

▲ A carp suffering from white spot.

POND FISH

Goldfish (*Carassius auratus*) in a choice of red, orange, yellow, and white permutations make an attractive addition to indoor ponds. They are easy to keep, so they are ideal for the beginner and for those just looking for color and movement in the water. There are also pedigree forms that feature classified modifications of the fins, body shape, tail, and coloring—shubunkins and comets, for example, or the attractive sarasa comet which has a white body and red head. There are even curiosities like the grotesque celestial with its bulbous body shape and fluid-filled sacs below wobbly eyes turned toward the ceiling. Goldfish are active swimmers, so they require good filtration and temperatures not exceeding 59°F (15°C). Other species worth considering include a shoal of rosy red minnows (*Pimephales promelas*) or the attractive silver-blue and orange shiners (*Notropis lutrensis*).

For really avid fishkeepers, koi—relatives of the humble goldfish that have been bred and selected over centuries for their size, color, and markings—are the kings. Despite their exotic appearance, they are hardy, so they can be kept in both indoor and outdoor pools. However, they do need special care and they grow to an extremely large size, so you need to calculate the size of your pond very carefully. Each requires a 10-foot swim and a minimum surface area of around 50 square feet (4.75sq.m). Koi dislike drastic changes in water temperature, so take this into account when planning which room you want to build your pool in. Generally, koi ponds should be around 5 feet (1.5m) deep. This would be impractical for a raised pond, but an indoor sunken pool of 3 feet (1m) deep with a raised wall of 2 feet (60cm) would make a good site for koi. Good filtration is essential to koi health, as they produce a lot of detritus; it is recommended that you contact a specialist supplier before buying filters and cleaners. You will also need to incorporate a bottom drain in your pond to remove fish waste regularly, and some form of shade should the pond be sited in a location which receives maximum sunshine. This might take the form of automatic blinds and shutters, or large foliage plants.

▲ The popular Red Shiner (*Notropis lutrensis*) is a slab-sided minnow with a terminal, oblique mouth.

Common goldfish

Shubunkin

▲ The Golden Fathead Minnow (*Pimephales promelas*). The dusky band or blotch in the front and rear rays of the dorsal fin helps distinguish these from other species of minnow.

Comet

► The lack of scale detail on the back of the Shusui koi differentiates it from the Asagi koi.

FITTING A BOTTOM DRAIN

Although you can install a bottom drain directly into the ground, it is better to lay a concrete base with the drain encased in it. This will form a suitable base for laying concrete blocks for a concrete pond, or a flexible liner as you choose. Liners for koi ponds are usually black, or a concrete finish which has been fiberglassed and painted black or dark green to show off the fish to their best advantage.

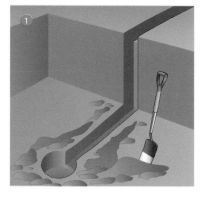

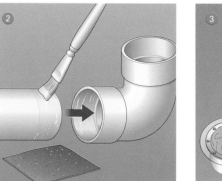

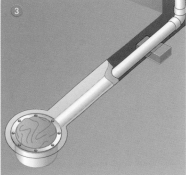

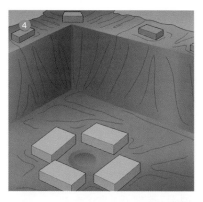

POINTS TO REMEMBER

● Always double-check your calculations at every stage of construction, as the components are expensive and mistakes impossible to rectify.

● Use good-quality components such as PVC or ABS plastic, which can be solvent welded together. The weld will be virtually instantaneous, so there is no leeway for adjustments.

● If pipework does not fit together easily "dry," rub the mating surfaces with abrasive paper until they slide together smoothly.

● Two or three pairs of hands are necessary for fitting the pipework together to prevent it from twisting out of place.

● When the drain pipework is in position and the concrete hardened, repeat the process to install a suitable filter system.

❶ Cut the pipework and fittings to size, double-checking your calculations and using a marker pen to show where the joints should be. Dig out the chamber for the pipework and the trenches for the pipe to run to an exterior drain.

❷ Now assemble the pipework *in situ*: clean both the male and female connections with solvent cleaner, then apply solvent cement to each jointing face. Insert one component into the other firmly without twisting. Leave for five minutes to strengthen before attaching the next component.

❸ Once all the pipework is fully fitted, it can be propped up with a piece of brick or block to make it level, then fixed permanently with a 4:1 concrete mix. Leave to set for several days.

❹ If you are finishing the inside of the pond with concrete, allow a slight slope toward the drain and aim for a minimum concrete depth of 6 inches (15cm). Pour it over evenly so that only the bottom drain is visible and the rest of the feed pipework to the filter is encased in concrete. Fitting a flexible liner to drain and pipework is more tricky and great care will be required not to tear the material. Line in the normal way (see pages 16 to 18) then pump out to a depth of about 12 inches (30cm). Position three or four concrete blocks carefully around the drain to prevent the liner from shifting. Now pump out the remaining water.

❺ Dry the liner around the drain area and rub a piece of chalk where you can feel the bottom drain flange beneath. This should produce an imprint of the center hole and screw holes. Cut the liner carefully around the center to expose the sump, holding the liner taut against the flange and cutting downward.

❻ Remove the circular section of liner and perforate the screw holes very carefully, using a punch. Clean all the mating surfaces and assemble the flange with mastic compound as supplied with the drain. Tighten the screws evenly.

AQUARIUM FISH

Not all fish are compatible, so check before you buy, and stay within the appropriate stocking levels. Some groups will cohabit happily enough, but will establish a kind of hiorarchy or pecking order, so that one species is more dominant than another. Make sure you select only freshwater fish, because marine species of fish and invertebrates require special aquarium conditions.

Butterfly fish
(*Pantodontidae*)

These quiet, hardy fish from tropical West Africa have an unusually shaped body and an upward-turned mouth. They prefer a slightly acid water and should not be kept with smaller species that live in the upper water layers, as they feed from the surface.

◀ A large, free-standing aquarium provides an excellent opportunity to observe fish at close quarters.

▼ You can keep a variety of fish in one tank if you make sure they are compatible.

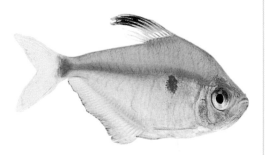

Characins
(*Characidae*)

This large family of more than a thousand species includes the popular tetras (*Hemigrammus* and *Hyphessobrycon*) from the Amazon basin, and the predatory piranha. All have teeth, and the right conditions—soft, slightly acid water—will best show off their brilliant colors.

Headstanders
(Anostomidae)

These are fish that swim vertically with their heads down and pick up food from the floor of the tank. They require a tank at least 39 inches (100 cm) long. Best known are the striped anostomus (*Anostomus anostomus*) and the spotted headstander (*Chilodus punctatus*), which grows up to 2½–3 inches (7–8 cm) long and should be kept as a shoal in a tank with a minimum length of 32 inches (80 cm) to prevent them from jumping out.

Barbs
(Cyprinidae)

This family includes a large number of fish suitable for a home aquarium, including danios, rasboras, and barbs. Most are distinguished by the one or two pairs of barbels on the lips. They are easy to keep and eat a wide range of foods.

Gyrinocheilidae

Gyrinocheilus aymonieri is popular because it consumes algae; one or two of these in an aquarium should be sufficient to keep it under control. They keep close to the bottom and prefer clear water rich in oxygen. Aim for a temperature range between 68 and 82°F (20 and 28°C).

Pencil fish
(Hemiodontidae)

This family of slender fish with teeth only in the upper jaw includes the beautiful three-banded pencil fish (*Nannostomus harrisoni*) and one-lined pencil fish (*Nannostomus unifasciatus*), which tend to remain motionless among dark plant cover. They prefer live food such as insect larvae.

Elephant trunk fish
(Mormyrids)

Despite their strange proboscis-like mouth, these exotic-looking fish are quite easy to keep, providing you do not have several specimens of the same species in the one tank. *Gnathonemus moorii*, for example, likes plenty of room and lots of rockwork and plant material to hide in. Keep the water as soft as possible and the lighting dim. These fish grow fast and may reach a length of 8 inches (20 cm).

Loach
(Cobitidae)

Loaches do well in an aquarium and include several species of *Acanthopthalmus*, which can reach a length of 3 inches (7.5 cm) and are active at dusk, remaining hidden during the day—ideal if you work away from home. The tiger loach (*Botia hymenophysa*) is more aggressive and should be kept only with other robust fish species. Clown loaches (*Botia macracantha*), which will appear during the day, are expensive but more peaceable.

Catfish

This is a huge group encompassing twenty families and more than 2,000 different species, many of which are too large for an aquarium. Most catfish tend to be active at night, but the armored catfish which grow only to about 2–4 inches (5–10 cm) long are more likely to be seen during the day. Some species like those in the genus Clarias are predatory so should not be kept in a tank with other fish. The glass catfish (*Kryptopterus bicirrhis*) is almost transparent and will grow to around 3 inches (10 cm) long. Always keep as a group, never as a single specimen. One of the most popular families of catfish is *Bunocephalidae*, which are small to medium sized with a large flat head and long thin tail.

Sunfish
(Centrarchidae)

One of the most popular sunfish is the pumpkinseed (*Lepomis gibbosus*), which can reach a length of 5½ inches (14 cm) and is easy to keep in a home aquarium. Sunfish can be kept in outdoor ponds, providing there is no risk of freezing.

Cichlids
(Cichlidae)

This is one of the main families of popular aquarium fish and contains a great number of species ranging from the magnificent discus to beautiful angelfish. Most species become extremely aggressive during breeding, so tankmates should be chosen with care and stocking levels (except for the Malawi cichlids) kept low. This group also includes discus—beautiful but quite difficult-to-keep fishes from South America—and their tank-bred varieties.

Toothcarps
(Cyprinodontidae, Poeciliidae)

Toothcarps tend to be predatory and can be beautifully colored. They require a generous surface area, so they prefer a wide flat aquarium, and they are good jumpers, so the tank needs a cover. They can be kept together with other species, providing there are no smaller or younger fishes in the tank. Swordtails, guppies, and platies are among the best-known live-bearing (i.e., not egg-laying) toothcarps (*Poeciliidae*), and these are good, adaptable fish for the aquarium beginner.

Labyrinth fish
(Anabantidae)

Labyrinth fish are specially adapted to take in bubbles of atmospheric air from the surface, as well as breathing underwater via their gills. The paradise fish (*Macropodus opercularis*) is possibly one of the first tropical fish to be introduced to Europe for keeping in an aquarium in 1876. It can grow to around 2½–3 inches (7–8 cm), but should not be kept with other species, as they may become aggressive. This group also includes the kissing gourami (*Helostoma temmincki*), whose fleshy lips, useful for grazing algae, give the impression they are kissing.

Nandids
(Nandidae)

The badis (*Badis badis*) is a popular aquarium fish growing up to 3 inches (8 cm) long and well colored. They may become aggressive toward one another in a tank, so provide plenty of good hiding places.

maintenance

The best way to keep an indoor garden looking good and in the peak of health is to maintain an efficient day-to-day regime of care and observation. That way, plants and fish get the best possible treatment as they need it, and any problems can be dealt with before they spread or worsen. If this does not seem to fit a busy working lifestyle, there are many basic maintenance functions such as shading and watering that can be controlled electronically, and a quick look over your garden at the end of the day can be a point of relaxation rather than a chore.

PLANT MAINTENANCE

Light, warmth, and water are plants' basic needs, and in the indoor garden it is your responsibility to supply all these in the right quantities. Familiarize yourself with individual plants' requirements and group the plants that enjoy the same environment. Your household heating system should be able to provide the necessary heating requirements; use thermostatically controlled electric heaters as a backup if necessary, bearing in mind that fan heaters are very drying on the atmosphere.

◀ A pebble mulch between plants looks good, and helps to preserve moisture in the soil.

MAINTENANCE TIPS

● Keep leaves, soil, and other plant detritus out of ponds and pools where they will pollute the water.

● In case of accidental spills from plants, ponds, or fountains, invest in a wet and dry vacuum cleaner that can quickly and safely deal with floods or leaks.

● Keep a card index or electronic notepad reminder of individual plants' needs—there is usually a card or label on new plants that details warmth, watering, and shade requirements.

Wet and dry vac

Card index system

HEBE

Thermometers

Watering can with long spout

Observe plants' lighting needs, too; natural light does not really penetrate far beyond the vicinity of the windows, and for plants to grow successfully you will need natural lighting bulbs, which also boost the shorter winter days. Decorative lighting can be used creatively to highlight larger foliage plants or to spotlight a pool or water ornament.

THE BEST WAY TO WATER

Under- and overwatering are the most common causes of plant failure. You need to get to know how much moisture your individual plants prefer and check regularly—the worst thing you can do is give everything a good soaking once a week. Use a small watering can with a long nozzle to prevent spills and a 1-quart (1-liter) plant sprayer for misting. Some plants prefer to be watered from the base, others like the leaves to be kept moist, and for some the compost must be allowed to dry out between each watering. Many species need very little water during their winter dormant period. As a general rule, a finger pressed on the soil surface will give some indication of whether watering is due: it should feel dry on top but moist below. Do not water if the surface is still damp. Soil moisture meters are available if you are unsure. Too often watering is inadequate; don't restrict each plant to a few drips but fill the space between compost and rim to ensure that the soil is well moistened.

If you have little time for watering or are going away on vacation, there are automatic watering systems available. These work best with plants that are grouped together on conservatory staging, on a shelf, or around a pool. The trickle system works by gravity, using a plastic, glass, or metal reservoir of water joined to small bore tubes by tee connectors. Each tube end is connected to a drip nozzle for controlling the water flow to individual plants. Alternatively, stand your plants on capillary matting which has been laid over plastic sheeting, its ends turned down into water reservoirs. The matting constantly absorbs water as required, which moistens the compost in the pots. You can make this system more efficient by inserting a "wick" of capillary material between the pot and matting.

Plants have differing humidity needs, too. Humidity is the amount of moisture in the air and is measured as Relative Humidity (RH) on a scale of 0 to 100. RH 0 percent is completely dry air; RH 100 percent is saturated

Trickle system

Capillary matting system

air. You can measure humidity with an hygrometer or moisture meter. Most plants prefer a relatively humid atmosphere—the exceptions are desert cacti, succulents, yuccas, and plants whose natural habitat is arid, desert terrain. As a rough guide, cacti and succulents need an RH of 35–40 percent, most houseplants prefer an RH of 60 percent, whereas delicate tropical plants flourish in an RH of around 80 percent. Naturally a pond or moving water feature in the room will help improve its general humidity, or you could purchase an electronically controlled automatic humidifier. Humid conditions are not necessarily comfortable for people, and you may prefer to install more localized forms of adding moisture to your plants. Standing pots in shallow trays of moist (not waterlogged) gravel or shingle works well; or you could insert pots in larger containers packed with moist peat, peat substitute, or a moist soilless mixture. In hot weather, plants could be sprayed regularly (preferably twice a day) with a mist sprayer. Do not mist cacti or plants with soft, felted foliage.

Feeding will also be necessary during the growing and flowering season: every two weeks is a good rule of thumb. Do not feed during a plant's dormant season. Plant food may be diluted in the watering can or added to the soil as sticks or pellets. Some plants require special formulations, which are available from garden centers and florists.

Hygrometer

Spray bottles for misting plants

TIP

Never feed a plant when the soil is dry; always water first.

◀ Plant food comes in a choice of easy-to-use formats.

▲ A terra-cotta pot makes a fine container for a sculptural copper cascade and complementary foliage plants.

BEDS AND POTS

While raised beds can be built in the conservatory and filled with appropriate compost for more permanent planting, most of your indoor plants will be in pots or containers. Submerged species should be planted in aquatic compost in hessian-lined baskets or specially designed underwater mesh pots. Floor- and shelf-standing plants might be in painted concrete planters, terra-cotta urns and pots, wooden tubs or color coordinated timber Versailles tubs, decorative ceramic cache-pots, even baskets, depending on the look you hope to achieve. It is a good idea to use standard plastic pots for your plants and insert them inside the more decorative

Colored glass stones

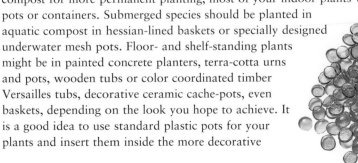

containers as this makes maintenance easier. Larger containers can be used to house a collection of more than one plant, providing they are compatible and are not allowed to crowd each other out. What is essential is that water or soil is not allowed to leak out and spoil your interior furnishings. Use saucers for all pots, lining them with pebbles for good moisture retention as well as decorative effect. Colored stones, which are available by the bag from aquarium stockists, look pretty in saucers and as a mulch on top of the soil; alternatively, use smooth glass-colored pebbles which can be bought from stores selling floral arrangement accessories.

Once your arrangement is established, regular watering, feeding, and de-bugging is essential to keep your plants in prime condition. Although there are automatic systems which can take over the chore of getting heat, light and warmth requirements right, it is important to keep a day-to-day eye on your plants as this will help pinpoint problems before they spread.

▶ Choose a style of container that best suits your tastes and interior decoration.

REPOTTING A PLANT

In time, plants will outgrow their container and no amount of feeding and watering will keep them looking good. They need repotting—preferably before the pot is tightly packed with roots. Most plants will need repotting about every two years. This should be done with care, ensuring that foliage and roots are not damaged. In between times, scrape away the top 2 inches (5cm) of soil and replace with fresh, to rejuvenate the plant. When repotting use the appropriate soil mixture for your plant. Any pots more than 6 inches (15cm) in diameter should be provided with broken pottery in the bottom for better drainage.

❶ Lift the plant out gently by the stem, supporting the foliage between your fingers, and easing the root ball out of the pot. Remove about 2 inches (5cm) of old soil from around the root ball and from the top of the plant. Trim the roots back by about the same amount.

❷ Put the plant in a larger, clean container of fresh soil, firm in, and water using a can with a many-holed nozzle to settle the compost around the roots.

POINTS TO REMEMBER

● Large plants in outsize containers may require two people to handle them. Place the pot or tub on its side with one person pulling the plant gently and the other tapping the rim firmly with a block of wood. A long flat blade run between the sides of the container and the root ball may also help shift a stubborn plant.

● The best time for repotting is midspring, or for dormant plants in winter.

● Repotting should be done before the container becomes tightly packed with roots.

● Pot up only into the next size container: too large and the plant will not flourish, as the roots stay too wet and may rot.

PLANT PESTS AND DISEASES

Early identification is your plant's best chance of survival. Remove disease- or pest-ridden parts from plants and treat immediately. Often two or more treatments will be necessary. If you are using chemical preparations, follow the manufacturer's instructions exactly and store in a cool, locked cupboard. Some sprays may carry a health warning. If the label does not say it is approved for indoor use, take the plant outside to treat and let the plant dry before bringing it back indoors. Never spray or treat plants near a pond or water feature, as there will be a risk of residue washing or dripping into the pond. Natural predatory controls, such as nematodes, ladybirds, and lacewing larvae, are available by mail at the appropriate time of year and can be very effective in an enclosed environment such as a conservatory.

COMMON PROBLEMS

▶ Consider introducing your own predators to keep summer bugs at bay.

Aphids

Look for: small insects often massed on stems or sucking sap on buds and soft growth; white flecks on leaves.

Treatment: spray with Retonone, soft or insecticidal soap, pyrethrum, or remove with a cotton swab with rubbing alcohol.

Scale insects

Look for: flat, shieldlike brownish insects on stems and leaves; honeydew.

Treatment: Remove with a soft, damp cloth. Spray with malathion or insecticidal soap. It is recommended to use malathion outdoors.

Powdery mildew

Look for: gray powder over foliage and flowers; drooping, distorted leaves.

Treatment: improve ventilation and prevent roots from drying out. Remove affected parts and spray or dust with fungicide, such as sulphur.

Red spider mites

Look for: tiny, pale orange mites on foliage; mottled, white leaves can look like webbing.

Treatment: improve humidity as red spider mite strikes in hot dry conditions. Spray with bifenthrin or insecticidal soap.

Whitefly

Look for: small white insects crowding the undersides of leaves. They fly up in clouds if you brush the foliage. Sticky honeydew residue.

Treatment: spray with pyrethrum, permethrin, or insecticidal soap.

Mealybugs

Look for: gray or pink insects with a fluffy white covering in plant crevices; sticky with honeydew.

Treatment: spray with malathion, pyrethrins labeled for indoor use, or insecticidal soap. It is recommended to use malathion outdoors when treating plants.

Downy mildew

Look for: yellow spots on leaf surface; gray mold below.

Treatment: thrives in cool, damp conditions so raise the temperature. Remove affected areas and spray with a fungicide.

Sooty mold

Look for: black sticky fungus; weak growth; spoiled flowers.

Treatment: wipe away the mold using a soft, damp cloth. Eradicate any sapsucking insects such as whitefly, scale insects, aphids, and mealybugs.

CONSERVATORY MAINTENANCE

A conservatory structure needs little maintenance apart from cleaning. You should be able to reach most areas both inside and out from a low stepladder or the window above, using a long-handled mop or squeegee. A crawling board with load-spreading timber beneath, supported by a bearer and adjustable prop, may be necessary to carry out repairs. Always take special care when working above glass, and get additional help if you can. To keep house tiles from slipping and smashing the panes in winter, a snow guard can be fitted above the gutters.

Check over the main frame and glazing bars once a year to detect signs of rot or areas that have begun to deteriorate. Painted or varnished finishes will probably need redoing annually. You should also check over the glazing; panes will have to be replaced if broken or cracked, although glazing tape is useful for temporary repairs. Sometimes the mastic or putty will have deteriorated; reseal with mastic or cover with self-adhesive flashing strip as a temporary repair.

HEATING AND COOLING

Inside the conservatory, your choice of plants will determine the environment you will be striving to maintain. Heating can be supplied as an extension of your existing central heating system providing it has the capacity. Radiators should be fitted with individual thermostats so that you can set to the necessary temperature. Alternatively, install a thermostatically controlled fan heater that takes up very little space and is extremely efficient, cutting in as required. Other options include electric tube heaters, which can be fitted unobtrusively below staging or shelving.

Shading from strong sunlight is equally important for the majority of plants and to prevent water features from greening over. Adjustable blinds, which can be fitted inside or outside the glass, are the most practical solution, and there is a wide range from which to choose, including slatted and decorative designs.

Ventilation will be necessary not just to aid coolness and oxygen in the summer months but, even more importantly, to prevent a stagnant, humid atmosphere in cold weather. Local building regulations may determine the number of vents installed. You need automatically controlled vent openers or thermostatically controlled extractor fans to combat poor ventilation when you are not there, or plants (and fish) may easily die. Some plant groups require high humidity. The old-fashioned way is to sluice the conservatory floor periodically with water; modern technology offers electronically controlled humidifiers that can be preset to your requirements.

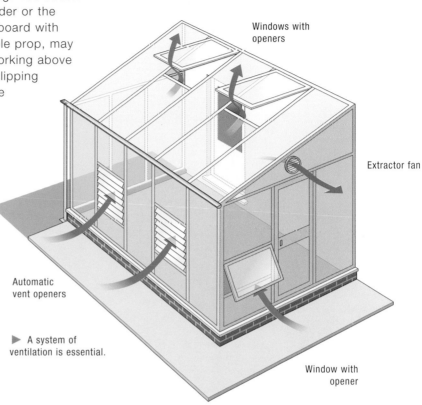

Windows with openers

Extractor fan

Automatic vent openers

▶ A system of ventilation is essential.

Window with opener

◀ Blinds can be used to control light and ventilation.

Slatted blind

Roller blind

TIP

If the conservatory makes access to house maintenance difficult, you can use a ladder to bridge the gap. Make sure you have someone at the bottom to hold it steady, and use a long extension ladder with plenty of overlap to make it sturdier.

POND MAINTENANCE

Indoor pool owners do not have to worry about outdoor water garden problems such as icing over, the predatory raccoon or heron, and dead leaves polluting the water in fall. However, higher temperatures (and predatory house cats!) can take their toll on pond linings and leaks may occur. In this event, you will have to drain the pool and repair it, using a proprietary repair kit depending on whether you have used flexible liner or concrete in the construction.

In the privileged environment of the conservatory or home, poolside plants will grow well and will have to be cut back. You are advised to grow aquatic and marginal plants in special underwater baskets so that they can be lifted and dealt with easily. Trim back roots and foliage or divide into new plants as appropriate. Replace in a container of fresh aquatic soil mix and lower gently into the pool: you must never drop suddenly.

High temperatures and good light levels may well result in an algae problem, especially in small pools. The installation of an ultraviolet (UV) filter will help to prevent algae, providing you have a filter to remove the dead algae. There are also chemical treatments designed to tackle this problem, and it is often a case of finding one that works for you. You must remove the dead material before it pollutes the water. Pond-balancing products and shading the surface of the pool with lilies and other aquatic plants may help redress the ecological balance.

▲ Special planting baskets are available for aquatic plants.

▲ Covering around two-thirds of the water's surface with aquatic plants like lilies will help prevent algae growth.

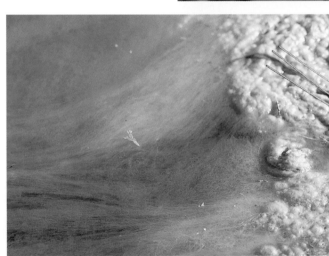

◀ ▲ Blanketweed will soon take over in warm, unshaded conditions. Use a stick or tool to twirl it out of the water.

◀ Pumps need regular maintenance in order to run efficiently.

Debris needs to be regularly removed from filters to prevent clogging; the UV sleeve needs cleaning and the bulb replacing annually. Pumps, ornaments, and other moving water features, including bubble fountains, should also be lifted and cleaned or serviced once a year as a matter of course. The pond itself should not need cleaning out too often. This is a major undertaking and one which should be tackled only if necessary. The warning signs are a drastic drop in water level indicating a leak, poor water quality, ailing plants, or unwell, maybe even dead fish. It is recommended that a total pond clean-up be undertaken in spring or early summer when fish and plants have a better chance of recovery.

CLEANING OUT THE POND

Unless it has been neglected or develops a serious problem, a small indoor pond or pool should need a complete cleaning out only every five years or so. Larger pools may be sufficiently balanced to need only minimum attention for ten years.

POINTS TO REMEMBER

● Get everything ready before you start, with suitable containers close at hand for fish, plants, and snails.

● Get help so that the procedure can be completed with minimum fuss as quickly as possible.

● Protect floors and furniture with plastic sheeting to avoid water damage.

● Tackle a clean-up only in spring or early summer to give plants and fish the summer season to recover.

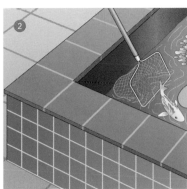

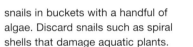

❶ Drain the pool by pumping, siphoning, or bailing it into the nearest outdoor drain or flower border. If the pond is raised, a length of hose no longer than 5 feet (1.5m) will be sufficient to siphon water to a lower level. Lay the hose in the pool so that it fills with water; hold one end in the water, covering the end with your thumb, and quickly lift the other end out of the pool to a lower level. If you remove your thumb as soon as the other end is lower than the surface of the pond, gravity will continue to draw out the water.

❷ Bail out the last few inches of water with a bucket so that you can sift the contents, removing any fish carefully with a net so that they can be transferred to a bucket or tank.

❸ Place fish, plants, and snails into separate containers of clean water. These should be at least 4–6 inches (10–15cm) deep—plenty of surface area is required to ensure high oxygen content. Plastic containers or buckets are ideal, providing they are clean and free from any detergent. Alternatively, if the job is going to take some time, transfer fish into a clean aquarium with some plant material for shelter; don't forget to feed if the clean-up isn't finished in a day. Keep snails in buckets with a handful of algae. Discard snails such as spiral shells that damage aquatic plants.

❹ When the pond is empty of water, sort out the plants. Water lilies can be kept in a bucket of water for up to a week, and marginal plants in their containers in a damp, shady spot, kept well watered. Submerged aquatics will need a bowl with enough water to cover them completely.

❺ Scoop out any remaining mud and debris, and scrub the sides and bottom of the pool with clean water, taking care not to damage the liner. Use a solution of potassium permanganate (making sure label instructions are followed) to remove stubborn stains—wear rubber gloves to keep the solution from staining your hands. Rinse the pool with clean water and allow it to dry before refilling. If using tap water, leave it for several hours for any chlorine to evaporate before returning plants and fish. Take this opportunity to trim and prune aquatic and marginal plants before replacing.

SUPPLIERS

UNITED STATES

Arizona
Green Thumb Garden Center
1200 Kanis Rd
Little Rock, AR 72211
Tel: 501-227-5454
Fax: 501-227-5491

California
Van Ness Water Gardens
2460 N. Euclid Ave
Upland, CA 91786
Tel: 909-982-2425
Fax: 909-949-7217

Mannion's Indoor Fountains
PO Box 632864
San Diego, CA 92163
Tel: 800-828-5967
Fax: 619-280-7711
www.buildfountains.com

Sunset Koi Fish Farm
33920 Travis Ct.
Menifee, CA 92584
Tel: 909-508-0722
Fax: 562-860-9310
www.koifish.com

Colorado
Spring Time Nursery
23902 County Rd. H
Sugar City, CO 81076
Tel: 719-267-4166
Fax: 719-267-4166
info@waterplants.com

Fountain Builder
1841 CR 977
Ignacio, Colorado 81137
Tel: 970-883-5346
info@fountainbuilder.com

Florida
Aquatics & Exotics Water Garden Nursery
1896 Walsingham Rd
Largo, FL 33778
Tel: 727-397-5532
www.aquaexotics.com

Fountains 'n' Slate
3841 Arbor Ave
Bunnell
FL 32110
Tel: 1-386-586-4062
Fax: 1-386-437-5733

Illinois
The Marine Connection
1111 W. Dundee Road
Wheeling, IL 60090
Tel: 847-520-7745
Fax: 847-520-9746

Indiana
Crystal Palace Perennials
PO Box 154
St. John, IN 46373
Tel: 219-374-9419
Fax: 219-374-9052
info@crystalpalaceperennials.com

Louisiana
Louisiana Iris
321 W. Main Street, Suite 2D
Lafayette, LA 70501
Tel: 337-232-6096
Fax: 337-233-5673
www.louisianairis.com

Maryland
Maryland Aquatic Nursery
3427 North Furnace Road
Jarrettsville, MD 21084
Tel: 410-557-7615
www.marylandaquatic.com

Massachusetts
Paradise Water Gardens
56 May Street, FN06
Whitman, MA 02382
Tel: 617-447-4711
Fax: 617-447-4591

Michigan
Ruby Conservatories
209 East Main Avenue
Zeeland, MI 49464
Tel: 616-772 3356
Fax: 616-772 5136
www.rubyconservatories.com

New Jersey
B&M Aquatic Garden & Koi Center
Route 94
Hamburg, NJ 07419
Tel: 201-209-1185
Fax: 201-827-4232

New Mexico
Lighted Fountains
(Glass Arts by Cole)
1509 Eastridge Dr. NE
Albuquerque, NM 87112
Tel: 505-323-0499
Fax: 505-323-0537
glassartsbycole@aol.com

New York
Scherer Water Gardens
104 Waterside Rd
Northport, NY 11768
Tel: 516-261-7432
Fax: 516-261-9325

Prosperity Fountain
PO Box 2486
Peter Stuyvesant Station
New York, NY 10009
Tel: 212-460-5624
mkeeler@rcn.com

North Carolina
Perry's Water Gardens
191 Leatherman Gap Rd.
Franklin, NC 28734
Tel: 704-524-3264
Fax: 704-369-2050

Ohio
Aquatic Technology
26966 Royalton Road
Columbia Station
OH 44028
Tel: 440-236-8330
Fax: 440-236-8336
Aquatictec@aol.com

Oklahoma
Water's Edge Aquatic Nursery
2775 Hardin Road
Choctaw, OK 73020
Tel: 405-737-0003
www.watersedgenursery.com

Oregon
Hughes Water Gardens
25289 SW Stafford Road
Tualatin, OR 97062
Tel: 503-638-1709
Fax: 503-638-9035
water@teleport.com

Pennsylvania
Overbrook Fountains
PO Box 733
Narberth, PA 19072
Tel: 610-704-8661
Fax: 215-877-5345
info@overbrookfountains.com

Renaissance Conservatories
132 Ashmore Drive
Leola, PA 17540
Tel: 717-661-7520
Fax: 717-661-7727

Tennessee
The Water Garden
5594 Dayton Blvd.
Chattanooga, TN 37415
Tel: 423-870-2838
Fax: 423-870-3382
e-mail: info@watergarden.com
www.thewatergarden.com

Washington
AquaDirect Corporation
AquaLink Executive Bldg
12815 Canyon Road E.
Suite T
Puyallup, WA 98373
Tel: 800–827-0117 / 253–538 2772
Fax: 253–538-2828

CANADA

Tropical Sunrooms
4487 Wellington Road South
London, Ontario N6E 2Z8
Tel: 1-888-606-6660/519-649-6543
www.tropicalsunrooms.com

UNITED KINGDOM

England
Aqua Inn Aquatic Centre
11 Midland Street
Barnsley
Yorkshire S70 1SE
Tel: 01226 733433

Aqua Logic
16-18 Walworth Road
London SE1 65P
Tel: 0207 703 8428

Aquasplash
MJS Garden Centre
Bath Road
Hare Hatch
Reading
Berkshire RG10 9SA
Tel: 01734 404188

Britain's Aquatic Superstores
225 Folds Road,
Bolton
Lancashire BL1 2TW
Tel: 01204 534343

Chenies Aquatics
Wyevale Garden Centre
Crown Lane
Farnham Royal
Buckinghamshire SL2 3SG
Tel: 01753 646989
Fax: 01753 642420

Chiltern Aquatics
Poplars Nursery
Harlington Road
Toddington
Bedfordshire LU5 6HE
Tel: 01525 875520

Derwent Koi & Tropicals
High Peak Garden Centre
Hope Road
Bamford, Nr Sheffield
Derbyshire S33 0AL
Tel: 01433 650029

Harmony Direct
(Conservatories)
229 Cricklewood Broadway
London NW2 3HP
Tel: 020 8208 0126
Fax: 020 8830 7498
e-mail sales@harmonydirect.co.uk
www.harmonydirect.co.uk

Interpet Limited
Vincent Lane
Dorking
Surrey RH4 3YX
Tel: 01306 881033
Fax: 01306 885009

North Lakes Aquatics
Robinson Street
Penrith
Cumbria CA11 9HR
Tel: 01768 891495

Rose Cottage Water Garden Centre
Glenside North
Pinchbeck
Spalding
Lincolnshire PE11 3SD
Tel: 01775 710882
Fax: 01775 710882
Email: Mike@rosecottagewgc.co.uk
www.rosecottagewgc.co.uk

Rugby Aquatics
91 Craven Road
Rugby
Warwickshire CV21 3JZ
Tel: 01788 543776

Smithdown Aquarium
357 Smithdown Road
Waver Tree
Liverpool L25 3JJ
Tel: 0151 733 1106

South Devon Water Gardens
Torbay Garden Centre
Brixham Road
Paignton
Devon TQ4 7BA
Tel: 01803 663355

Stapeley Water Gardens
Nantwich
Cheshire CW5 7LH
Tel: 01270 628628
Fax: 01270 624188

The Aquatic Centre
200 Kingston Road
North End
Portsmouth
Hampshire PO2 7LR
Tel: 01705 666640

The Complete Aquatic Centre
190 Stockport Road
Altrincham
Manchester
M34 6AU
Tel: 0161 904 0724

The Waterlife Studio
Booker Garden Centre
Clay Lane
Booker
Marlow
Buckinghamshire SL7 3DH
Tel: 01494 526865

Wildwoods Water Gardens
Theobalds Park Road
Crews Hill
Enfield
Middlesex EN2 9BP
Tel: 020 8366 0243
Fax: 020 8366 9892
info@wildwoods.co.uk

World of Water Aquatic Centres
(13 locations UK-wide)
www.worldofwater.co.uk

Scotland
Barnacle Aquatics Inc.
(mail-order only)
P.O. Box 661
West Dundee
Tel: 847 428-0018
Fax: 847428-0018
Email: barnacle@barnacle-
aquatics.com
www.barnacle-aquatics.com

The Aquatic Centre
15-17 Comely Green Place
Edinburgh EH7 5SY
Tel: 0131 468 2585

Wales
Aquajardin
Hurrans Garden Centre
Catsash Road
Longstone
Nr Newport
Gwent NP18 2LZ
Tel: 01633 413587

Seaworld Aquatics
9 Kinmel Street
Rhyl
Denbighshire LL18 1AE
Tel: 01745 342228

AUSTRALIA

Wallis Creek Water Gardens
Wallis Creek Lane
Mulbring
N.S.W. 2323
Tel: (02) 4938 0230
Email: fenech@aljan.com.au

Water Garden Paradise Aquatic
Nursery (mail-order)
P.O.Box 7039
Bass Hill
N.S.W. 2197
www.freeyellow.com

NEW ZEALAND

Wrights Watergardens
154 Mauku Road
RD 3
Pukekohe
New Zealand
Tel: 064 9 2363642
Fax: 064 9 2363642
Email: wriwatgdn@xtra.co.nz

Cedarlite Nationwide
(Conservatories)
9A Sylvia Park Business Centre
286 Mt Wellington Highway
Auckland
Tel: 9-573-5533
Fax: 9-573-1605
e-mail info@cedarlite.co.nz
www.cedarlite.co.nz

INDEX

CREDITS

Quarto would like to thank and acknowledge the following for supplying pictures reproduced in this book:

Key: b = bottom, t = top, c = center, l = left, r = right.

Ailsa Direct 11 tr, 48 cr, 135 tc. **Dave Bevan** 19 tr, 92bl, 115 tr, 116 tl, tcl, tr, tcr, 122 bcr, 123 bl, tr, br, 124 tl, 125 tr, 126 tr, bc, 127 br, tr, c, 129 tr, 131 tc, 136 tr, 138 tr, c. **Bradstone** 29 tr, 44 br, 68 br, 84 br, 100 cr, 108 bl. **Ceramica de Catalunya** 6 br, 79r, 135 cr. **Chenies Aquatics** 14 tr, 44 bl. **Effect-Line Aquarium from CASCO Europe** 129 tl. **Farmer Foster** 84 tr. **Forest Garden** 6 t, 135 tr. **Garden Picture Library** 7 (photo Jane Legate), 10 l (photo John Glover, designer Chenies Aquatics), 17 tr (photo Ron Sutherland, designer Anthony Paul), 20 tr (photo Clive Nichols, designers Paul Thompson/Trevyn McDowell), 28-9 tc (photo Christopher Gallagher), 35 (John Glover), 72 tc (Lynne Brotchie), 75 (Lynne Brotchie), 84 tc, 87(Tim Griffith), 95 (John Miller), 96 t (Ron Sutherland). **Glass Block Technology** 91 rct, rcc, rcb. **Goblin** 132 cr. **Haddonstone** 45 bl, 79 c, 135 ctr. **Harpur Garden Library** 88 tc, 91 l (Luciano Giubbilei). **Haws Watering Cans** 133 tr, 134 tc, cr. **Interpet** 16 tr, 18 tl, tc, 20 tl, bl, 24 tc, tr, bc, 68 bl, 94 br, 105 tl, 124 bl, 125 tr, 126 tl, cl, bl, 138 tl, cr. **Stephen C Markham Collection** 15 tr, cr, 72 rc, 135 c. **Maryland Aquatic Nurseries** 52bl (Bob Romar). **Peter McHoy** 64 tl. **Clive Nichols** 2-3 (des: Michael Cedar), 15 bl (Stephen Woodhams), 30-31 (des: Wynniatt-Husey Clarke. **Oase** 18r, 20tc, c, 21 tl, tc, 48 bl, 64tr. **Ocean Outdoor** 88 blt, blb. **Jerry Pavia Photography** 79 l. **Photomax** 24br, 80 tc, 83, 125 br. **Pisani** 104 tr, cr. **Reef One** 80 bl. **Eric Sawford** 118 tl, crb, clt, 119 clt, br, 120 tr, bcl, 121 tl, tr, 122 bl, tcr. **The Silk Plant Company** 56 br. **Harry Smith Horticultural Photographic Collection** 27 tr, 44 tc, 47. **Stapeley Water Gardens** 21 tr, 115 br, 125 bl, 138 bl. **Peter Stiles** 117 tl, tcr, 118 crt, tr, br, 119 crt, 120 bl, bcr, br, 121 tcl, tcr, bcl, bcr, br, 122 tl, bcl, 123 bcr, 132 bl. **Stowasis** 8 tr, 11 tl, 14 br, 32 bl, 40 bl, 104 br, 134 bl. **Nicola Stocken Tomkins** 100 t (Designer Gaila Adair). **Touchwood European** 101 tl, tcl, 108 br. **Town & Country Conservatories** 9 b. **Waterford Gardens** 96 bl, 129 bl. **West Meters** 23 br 134 tr.**Elizabeth Whiting Associates** 8 bl, 104 tc, 108 t, 111.

Special thanks go to Su Chin for use of her bonsai design on pages 52–55.

All other photographs and illustrations are the copyright of Quarto. While every effort has been made to credit contributors, we apologize in advance if there have been any omissions or errors

CONTACT DETAILS

CASCO Europe Ltd; www.casco-group.com
Ceramica de Catalunya (Tel +44 (0)1491 628994 for nearest stockist)
The Silk Plant Company www.silkplant.co.uk, email sales@silkplant.co.uk